[redacted]

Hoffman, Carl, 1952-

The Punan

[redacted]

The Punan
Hunters and Gatherers of Borneo

Studies in Cultural Anthropology, No. 12

Conrad Phillip Kottak, Series Editor

Professor of Anthropology
The University of Michigan

Other Titles in This Series

No. 2	*Inuit Behavior and Seasonal Change in the Canadian Arctic*	Richard G. Condon
No. 3	*The Marquesan Notion of the Person*	John Kirkpatrick
No. 4	*Matrilocal Residence in Pre-Literate Society*	William Divale
No. 5	*Factory Women in Taiwan*	Lydia Kung
No. 6	*Nutritional Strategies and Agricultural Change in a Mexican Community*	Kathleen Musante DeWalt
No. 7	*Umbanda: Religion and Politics in Urban Brazil*	Diana DeG. Brown
No. 8	*Work and Power in Maale, Ethiopia*	Donald L. Donham
No. 9	*The Miyanmin: Human Ecology of a Papua New Guinea Society*	George E. B. Morren, Jr.
No. 10	*Mothers of Money, Daughters of Coffee: The* Wok Meri *Movement*	Lorraine Sexton
No. 11	*Himalayan Households: Tamang Demography and Domestic Processes*	Thomas E. Fricke

The Punan
Hunters and Gatherers of Borneo

by
Carl Hoffman

UMI RESEARCH PRESS
Ann Arbor, Michigan

This study was supported in part by United States National Institutes of Health National Research Service Award 5 F31 MHO7995-03.

Produced and distributed by
UMI Research Press
an imprint of
University Microfilms, Inc.
Ann Arbor, Michigan 48106

Library of Congress Cataloging in Publication Data

Hoffman, Carl, 1952-
The Punan : hunters and gatherers of Borneo.

(Studies in cultural anthropology ; no. 12)
Revision of author's thesis (Ph.D.)—University of Pennsylvania, 1983.
Bibliography: p.
Includes index.
1. Punan (Bornean people) I. Title. II. Series.
DS646.32.P85H63 1986 306'.0899922 86-7071
ISBN 0-8357-1750-X (alk. paper)

Stare a long time at something strange,
and its strangeness will disappear.

Chinese Proverb

Contents

Figures

Acknowledgments

This study was made possible through the support of the United States National Institutes of Health and through the approval and cooperation of Lembaga Ilmu Pengetahuan Indonesia (LIPI). I am deeply grateful for their assistance.

The field research underlying this study could not have been accomplished without the help and hospitality of countless people in Indonesia, for whom "taking care of strangers" is a deeply embedded fact of life. I thank them for their friendship and astonishing kindness.

1

The "Punan Problem": An Introduction

In essence, this study is intended to be a critical look at a peculiar idea. It involves the examination of a mental image that has persisted in the minds of many for well over one hundred years—the idea of the "Wild People of the Woods," the so-called "Punan" of Borneo. And in our analysis of this fanciful image, we shall be led to approach certain issues that are larger than that of the Punan themselves.

There is and has been a vivid, time-honored, and rather colorful conception of a type of people on the island of Borneo who are known as Punan. Four generations of Western travelers, traders, colonial officials, and anthropologists have been fascinated by the very idea that such people could exist.

In its general outlines, the prevailing conception has depicted an extraordinarily primitive, nomadic, hunting and gathering people, widely dispersed in small groups scattered across the length and breadth of Borneo, wandering about in the deepest recesses of the jungle, sleeping in caves and in "rude shelters" of sticks and leaves, sickened by direct sunlight, afraid of other people, seldom seen and hard to find, and considered to be barely human "savages" by the headhunting Dayak tribes of the longhouses and villages. The notion that somewhere within the "dark inner forests" of Borneo there lives a people somehow more primitive than the primitive, more savage than the savage, and more hidden than the already remote Dayak tribes has been an idea that has appealed persistently to something very deep in the minds of Western visitors to Borneo.

It cannot be said with certainty when exactly it was that the Punan first became known to Europeans, although it is certain that decades of rumors preceded actual encounters. While initial European trading activity in Borneo established some familiarity with sedentary, village-dwelling, agricultural Dayak tribes* as far back as the late eighteenth century, it was not until the middle of the nineteenth century that the world began to hear of the Punan.

*The term Dayak will be used throughout this study in its broadest sense, recognized formerly in Dutch Borneo and presently in Indonesian Borneo as referring to all of the indigenous, proto-Malay, tribal peoples of the island's interior.

Among the earliest descriptions of Punan to appear in print was one presented in 1882 by the explorer and naturalist Carl Bock, who encountered a small group of these people during a brief journey up the Mahakam River.

> I was intending to penetrate into the forest and endeavour if possible to solve for myself the mystery of the Orang Poonan, or Wild People of the Woods....
>
> We started at sunrise, taking a small prau up the river—the Poonan chief, myself, Sariman, and four of the tribe. After paddling some twenty miles up the stream, the canoe was turned to the left into a narrow creek, up which we proceeded for a couple of hours. Suddenly the prau was stopped, and the Poonan made signs that we must land and go through the forest. I could see no trace of a landing-place; and, though I had kept an anxious look-out for any indications of human habitation, I had seen none. There was nothing to show that the spot at which we had stopped was different from any other point throughout the whole distance we had travelled—no trace of a path, not even a broken branch or other indication of traffic could I see, as a sign that human foot had ever trodden there before. I was afterwards told that the Poonans made marks on trees to show their movements and resting places to each other. After struggling through a bamboo thicket, which, to all appearance, had never before been disturbed by human hand or foot, we found ourselves in the dense forest. The chief made a curious cry, *Hio! hio!* which was answered by another voice in the distance; and a few minutes later I was led up to a tall tree, where, sitting under an awning of attap, supported by four bamboo sticks, were three young women, one of them with a baby in a sort of cradle slung on her back; while a fourth woman, much older, was roasting the thick hide of a long-nosed monkey (*nasalis larvatus*) before a fire. Just beyond were two men, who came forward as we approached.
>
> My stay among these primitive wild people of the woods was limited to a single afternoon.... (Bock, 1882:69-70, 71)

And yet, in that single afternoon, Carl Bock managed to accomplish something that most of us only dream about. For better or for worse, he gave birth to an idea that has persisted right down to the present day. Bock formulated an opinion of the Punan that has remained the basis of our conception of them ever since: "I believe these savages to be the true aborigines of Borneo. They live in utter wildness in the central forests of Borneo, almost entirely isolated from all communication with the rest of the world" (ibid.:76).

Having been established as the basic paradigm, Bock's views were quickly echoed. Charles Hose, speaking from experience with Punan groups of the Baram district in northern Sarawak, declared, "I have no doubt in my mind that this wandering race of people are the aboriginals of the country" (1893:157). Hose subsequently went on to claim that the Punan "do not count beyond three" (Hose and McDougall, 1912, II:211).

As the years went by, the conception was embellished. This description of Punan by one Mervyn Beech appeared in no less a medium that the journal *Man*:

Inche Abdallah bin Nakhodah is my authority for the following information concerning these weird people. He is a Malay trader of Tawao. The Punans live in the dense jungle beyond the Sagai in the interior of Bolongan, on the east coast of Borneo. They are a hunter tribe (corresponding somewhat to the Dorobo of East Africa), and will not come into a village, but always live in the jungle, as they are unable to bear the heat and glare of the sun.... They wear no clothes except the bark of trees; they have no houses or property, but wander about and sleep in trees. They are rapidly becoming extinct....

They have a curious method of leaping three or four yards at a time, instead of walking, and their celerity of movement is astounding.

Those who have had the opportunity of seeing the [sic] dance have told me that the performance is quite marvellous, their bodies seeming to be made of elastic and to contain no bones. (Beech, 1911:17)

And from the *Journal of the Malayan Branch of the Royal Asiatic Society,* we have these observations on "The Gypsies of Sarawak" by a Captain E.L. Andreini:

To find these interesting and delightful people you must desert the highways and even byeways of Sarawak and delve into the heart of the jungle land, the haunt of the bear and barking deer, the wild cat and argus pheasant; you must travel up and down many little streams, the beginning perhaps of mighty rivers, whilst overhead you may hear the sound of the great Hornbill as he flies from his feeding ground back to the giant trees that serve for his home. All the time you will have the feeling that unseen eyes are watching you and so indeed they may be—for Punans are timid people and greatly fear the roving Sea Dyak and it is said they have the art of camouflage in its most perfect form. From behind trees motionless people will watch your progress and later will astonish you, in their encampment, by informing you that they saw you pass such and such a place the same morning whilst you yourself and your followers have seen nothing....

A people of the jungle living very much like animals, hunting and with the fear of the hunted in their hearts. One leaves their primitive encampment with the thought that here is a link with man's origin, but realizing what tremendous progress man has made since our forefathers too lived the life of the hunter, and with pity in one's heart for these simple people who are slowly, like the wild beast, being exterminated by the ravages of man and diseases. (Andreini, 1924:76-77)

A new element was added subsequently by Charles C. Miller, a Hollywood cameraman traveling around the upper Mahakam and Kayan rivers. In this description the Punan, hitherto depicted as timid and fearful of other people, now became "the nomadic gangsters of the jungle. Rough, tough, and physically fearless, they will run only from spirits" (Miller, 1942:facing p. 263).

There are three tribes in Borneo seldom visited by white men, partly because they have no home in which to be visited, but mainly because they are so tough, so cold-blooded and so utterly fearless that they would regard a social visit as an open invitation to murder. These nomadic gangsters of the jungle are called the Hebans, the Punans and the Bukats, and among the three of them they have Borneo pretty evenly divided.

> If three bands of man-eating tigers decided to divide up a country, the result would be pretty much the same.... Unseen and unheard, they slink through the jungle on silent feet, moving swiftly from one camp to another, seldom staying in the same place more than a few nights and getting nowhere. They don't want to get anywhere; it is enough that they get away from the place they last were. It is hardly an exaggeration to say that their children are born under dry leaves, cradled in the tree tops, and weaned on panther milk. At the age of six a Punan youngster will run down a monkey in its own tree-top, and at the age of ten will walk up to a wild boar and spit betel-nut juice in its eye. By the time a youth reaches manhood he will already have killed with a blow-gun. They are tough. Not many of them reach manhood....
>
> All the way up the Mahakam, across to the Apo-Kajan and back to the Barito I was on the lookout for the roving killers, but all we heard of them were rumors....
>
> Their big ace in the hole is the cowardice of the stay-at-home tribes. A rajah needing more slaves will often employ a Punan tribe to do a little kidnapping for him... or he might employ the Punans to bring him fresh human heads to replenish the fading magic of his old collection....
>
> There is no way of getting in touch with the Punans or the other nomad tribes on their own grounds, but when wanted they always seem to appear. A rajah has but to think longing thoughts of a new force of slaves and suddenly when he is alone near the edge of the *kampong* he will find himself staring into the intent brown eyes of a Punan. The rajah does not cry out. He knows that all around him, invisible in the brush, are the blow-guns of a dozen warriors, and when these boys puff a dart, they don't miss....
>
> Under the circumstances it can be seen that the settled tribes regard the nomads with terror, as well they might. "Go to sleep or the Punans will get you," is a sure way to frighten a Dyak baby into a state of hysterical wakefulness. (Miller, 1942:266-70)

Thus by the eve of the Second World War, the Punan had already achieved a rather well-developed persona in the minds of those familiar with the island of Borneo. And in sixty short years they had somehow managed to progress—or perhaps retrogress—from Bock's "Wild People of the Woods" to Miller's "nomadic gangsters of the jungle." The subject was obviously ready for some clarification at the hands of "real" anthropologists. As it happened, however, such discussion as there was by anthropologists in the 1940s succeeded only in making the subject a bit murkier.

Whereas much of the writing up to this point had so graphically described a people who logically could not have existed outside the imagination, anthropologist Fay-Cooper Cole asserted in 1945 that the "Punan" in fact *did not* exist outside of our imagination.

> It is certain that... these authorities and others did see people called "punan," but the writer is inclined to doubt their existence as a distinct people. In central Borneo any party gathering jungle products and making temporary camps is known as "punan" or campers. (Cole, 1945:99)

As an added touch, Cole went on to suggest the possibility that anthropologists and other travelers to Borneo had been misled into believing in the existence of the Punan as a distinct people due to a simple "misunderstanding." This misunderstanding, Cole offered, was created by "the many abandoned shacks one sees in the jungle," causing observers to deduce incorrectly the existence of a distinct jungle people (ibid.).

Cole's analysis of the Punan met with little support; indeed it was almost immediately challenged. As Robert Heine-Geldern remarked the following year:

> The merest outlines only are known of the nomadic and truly primitive Punan. . . . Recently even doubts of the existence of the Punan as a distinct people have been expressed by Fay-Cooper Cole. . . . These doubts are wholly unfounded. The Punan have been seen, described, and photographed by numerous observers. (Heine-Geldern, 1946:161)

Unpersuaded, Cole responded to Heine-Geldern a year later in a letter to the *American Anthropologist*:

> I wish to take exception to the sentence "These doubts are wholly unfounded." Despite the fact that people called Punan have been seen and reported by reliable parties I am still inclined to doubt their existence as a distinct people. . . .
>
> I went to Borneo looking for Punan. While in Central Borneo I sought in vain for any such people, but I did find that any group which was away from home gathering jungle products and living in temporary camps was known as *punan*. I saw several such Punan groups but upon inquiry found they all related to fixed villages. Under the circumstances I believe that in Central Borneo the term has no other significance than our word "camper." It is possible that in Sarawak and elsewhere there may be truly nomadic Punan, but for the moment I think there is reasonable doubt that this is true. (Cole, 1947:340)

Cole's doubts about the Punan were not shared by others, however. His statements were rather promptly dismissed by anthropologists and others familiar with Borneo, and they have indeed been regarded as a radical position ever since.

Among the majority of those familiar with Borneo's peoples and cultures, the one point that was certain in the 1940s was the same point that was evident in the days of Carl Bock, namely that there *were* genuine, full-time groups of hunters and gatherers in Borneo called Punan. And, all of the colorful and often fanciful notions about them notwithstanding, they were somewhat peculiar in that "they deviated from other Malayan peoples in being nomadic" (Cole, 1947:340). As such, the question that began to emerge in these years was not whether the Punan really existed, but rather who the Punan were and what they were really like.

The crux of the problem was enunciated in 1949 by the late Tom Harrisson, who was at that time Government Ethnologist of Sarawak.

> No outside investigator has ever made a protracted study of any Punan group, and we do not even know if the persons so termed really represent a culturally, a linguistically or physically related people, or whether they have several origins and are uniform only in a common habit of nomadism. (Harrisson, 1949:131)

Harrisson noted that other peoples of Borneo's interior had their own theories as to the origins of the Punan—that they are simply the descendants of runaway slaves, criminals, social misfits, and wrong-doers from settled tribes—and he suggested, "There is reason to think that at least this was a source of addition, accretion, to Punan bands" (ibid.:133). But as for the origin of the bands themselves, Harrisson said,

> [T]he present writer thinks it likely, from his study of old legends and particularly of war stories, that whole villages of weak or overwhelmed groups may have "gone bush" in despair, too—as in the periods of great Kayan and Iban expansion during the last century. (Ibid.)

It was during the succeeding decade that several groups of these people finally became the object of a protracted field study by a professionally trained social anthropologist. Rodney Needham conducted two field studies in Sarawak, in 1951-52 and 1958, and contributed solid and significant ethnographic insight into such topics as social organization (1954a, 1965, 1971), religion and cosmology (1964), and the relationship between ecological pressures and basic human drives (1954b). He also put forward a brief but thorough general ethnographic profile of the groups that he studied (1972), that has since become a sort of basic working paper on the Punan. The net effect of all of these publications has been to move the Punan out of the realm of myth and into the realm of science.

Particularly significant, however, were Needham's observations concerning the ethnic heterogeneity of the various "Punan" groups. Needham maintained that the people he studied referred to themselves as Penan and considered themselves culturally, historically, and linguistically distinct from groups known as Punan. Moreover, he discovered that the term *Punan* was used in Sarawak to refer not only to nomadic groups but also to some longhouse people as well, namely the Punan Ba (1954c, 1955). Finally, Needham noted that even within the classification Penan, there were some evident distinctions:

> They compose two tribes, Eastern and Western, separated in the main by the Baram River. Although the tribes recognize each other as true Penan, i.e. as culturally similar forest nomads, there are marked differences between them. These linguistic and social disparities are sufficient to justify the ethnographical separation of the Eastern and the Western Penan into two distinct societies. (1972:177)

Needham's distinction between Punan and Penan promptly led to what Harrisson (1975:4) called an "absurdly amusing" debate over whether the two terms really reflect ethnic differences or are merely the result of dialect variation in the pronunciation of the same word. Herbert Whittier argued

> In Sarawak there may be a case for a distinction between "Punan" and "Penan"; in Kalimantan, however, I found that some Kenyah groups referred to the "nomads" as "Penan" while other Kenyah groups referred to the same group as "Punan." The distinction "Penan/Punan" here seems to be a matter of dialect differentiation among the Kenyah groups. (1974:42)

Harrisson added:

> As Whittier points out for Kalimantan, so it is—and always was—for Sarawak too: the distinction in vowel sounds is in the beholders. One and the same group may be called Penan by some (settled) group and Punan by another adjacent (settled) group. Where the Kayans dominate, Penan probably rules? Most Kenyan [sic] and others, including all earlier European writers, prefer Punan. For any serious student to base ethnic classification on such flimsy semantics is naif, if not faintly frivolous. (1975:4)

This enduring debate—Punan versus Penan—has persisted to the present day. It seems that if indeed there is anything absurdly amusing about it, it is simply that both sides of the argument are probably correct. It is reasonable to suppose, on the one hand, that dialectical variation probably was the initial factor in the emergence of the two variant terms. On the other hand, Needham's own observations in the field seem to indicate that the Punan/Penan distinction is sociologically real and meaningful to the "Penan" themselves:

> Until 1951 no white man had ever spoken the Penan language, and when they are asked about the name "Punan" the Penan smile and say: "The white men do not know our language, and this is the name they have given us. The Punan are certainly a different people. We are Penan." (Needham, 1954c:82)

As we shall see in the course of this study, Needham's assertions that the "Eastern Penan" are distinct from the "Western Penan," that both of these are different from nomadic "Punan," and that these in turn are unrelated to the settled Punan Ba would seem to suggest that Needham was onto something important.

In this regard, Needham was not alone. During the many years that intervened since Carl Bock's early encounter with the "Orang Poonan," a small handful of individuals—mostly colonial officials of one sort or another—were quietly publishing papers that suggested the possibility that the "Punan" are not quite what they appear at first glance. We shall have occasion to review these scattered observations in their proper context, throughout chapter 3. The point to be raised now, however, is that these papers were by and large narrow-focused studies of specific regions. Dealing mostly with a particular Punan group in a particular locale, these studies did not lend themselves readily to a general understanding of the "Punan problem."

As a result, the persistent image of the "Wild People of the Woods" has remained alive and intact to the present moment, as evidenced in these descriptions appearing in the last decade:

> The Penan are thought to be possibly the group most indigenous to Sarawak, altho [sic] some likely come from Kalimantan, and they might have come in silent bands from almost anywhere....
>
> In their relative fairness and delicacy, graceful quickness, and attentiveness to nature, they remind me of an aspect of the Balinese. But that is likely no further off the mark than any other guess about the mysterious Penan. A perhaps romantic notion is that they are a group that was marked by others and themselves as a "holy" group, like a Hindu type of wandering group that is bound to an ethic of self-sufficiency within nature, supplicants, possession being anathema....
>
> The expression of the eyes is clear and somewhat distant, a paradox of the "direct non-look." The aspect of the entire being is one of attentiveness, as if one were always listening in an alert dream state....
>
> Then we had to leave the elusive Penan. The gekko lizards, charming and wriggling, come to mind, and trackprints and imprints of lizards found among layers of stone—a past and present that is one, somehow remaining in mid-movement....
>
> More than any other group, despite my affection for each group for its own ways, I felt that the Penan I met and lived among were of an especially high order spiritually. (Rubenstein, 1973:1330-37)

> The Punan: These tribesmen are the original inhabitants of Borneo who even precede the Dayaks. Very elusive aboriginals, the Punans run when they *smell* you coming.... Their features are more Mongolian than the Dayaks' and the Dayaks consider them savages.... It's better if you arrange to go with a government party, they could be defensive and hostile. They are fearless because they don't know any better.... (Dalton, 1977:352)

The fact that such depictions as these could continue to appear at this rather late date probably results from the relative neglect of Borneo by social scientists. Stated simply, Borneo has not received its due share of attention by anthropologists. George Appell, remarking some years ago on the "singular lack of social-anthropological research undertaken there," observed:

> While social-anthropological research in Borneo at present may comprise two to three projects per year, the average rate since World War II has been about one and a half. This compares unfavorably with research in New Guinea, for example, which, although it is somewhat larger in geographic size, has a smaller population. Yet, just in that half of the island that encompasses the Trust Territory of Papua-New Guinea, research there has been averaging about sixty field projects per year.... (Appell, 1976:1)

Yet, even if we are forced to resign ourselves to this overall neglect of Borneo as an unfortunate fact of life, our continuing lack of knowledge and our misconceptions about the Punan are nonetheless inexcusable. The Punan are hunters and gatherers, and this alone ought to be enough to move them considerably nearer to center stage. The study of hunting and gathering peoples has been a major, ongoing concern of anthropology for many years, and it is likely to remain so. As we shall see in the course of this study, the Punan of Borneo have some interesting things to teach us on the subject of hunting and gathering as a way of life.

In the following pages, we shall be concerned primarily with trying to determine just who exactly these Punan are and what they mean in terms of the ethnographic picture of Borneo as a whole. In our attempts to answer these questions, we shall be led inevitably to consider certain issues of larger scope that go beyond the Punan themselves. We shall likely be afforded some new perspectives on the history of insular Southeast Asia, on the historical significance of Borneo itself, and—perhaps most important—on the persistence of the hunting and gathering adaptation to the present day.

Before we begin to confront these issues, however, let us first examine the Punan ethnographically—precisely as they appear.

2

Punan: A Descriptive Overview

Distribution

Groups of present and former nomadic hunters and gatherers known as Punan (or Penan) are widely distributed across the island of Borneo. They are present in all but one of the four provinces of Indonesian Borneo, throughout much of Sarawak, and in Brunei. There are presently no known Punan groups in Sabah.

The ethnographic situation is complicated somewhat by the fact that there are groups called Punan which are not nomadic, and which have no tradition of ever having been nomadic. Aside from the previously noted Punan Ba, there are the Punan Biau and the Punan Tepaling of the Belaga district in Sarawak, who have been described as "longhouse dwellers and sophisticated agriculturalists," for whom "there is no evidence, within living memory, to indicate that they were nomads" (Langub, 1975:45). There are, in addition, several nomadic groups who are known by names other than Punan or Penan. In Sarawak these groups have been referred to by such terms as Ukit, Bukit, Bukitan, Bukat, Pakatan, and Sian, among others. In Indonesian Borneo, or Kalimantan as it is now called, there is a group known variously as Kareho and Penyabung who were nomadic until roughly sixty years ago; there are, moreover, two groups who are presently nomadic known as Basap. It may be noted, however, that the overwhelming majority of nomadic groups in Borneo are referred to as Punan or Penan, and that in Indonesian Borneo the term of reference is almost always Punan.

Between August 1980 and November 1981 I conducted an ethnographic survey on Punan groups in Kalimantan. My search for these people took me to several widely scattered areas in the provinces of East and Central Kalimantan. I did not have the opportunity to visit Punan groups in the province of West Kalimantan and there are no Punan in the province of South Kalimantan.

The ensuing descriptive remarks derive from my visits.

Punan Batu, Punan Binai, Punan Sajau

The Punan Batu are a nomadic group that ranges around the headwaters of the Sajau River in the coastal district of Tanjung Palas, in the Bulungan Regency.* *Batu* is the Malay word for stone, and the name of this group derives from the many limestone caves at the upper Sajau, in which these people gather birds' nests and sometimes seek shelter.

A segment of this group has recently branched out into the Binai River—a small tributary of the Sajau—and are now called the Punan Binai. These people, roughly fifteen nuclear families in all, continue to maintain close contact with members of the parent group; intermarriages are still common.

Another portion has for some eighteen years been settled in a village on the lower Sajau, where they have taken up rice agriculture. This group is referred to as the Punan Sajau, but its composition is somewhat fluid. The village was established, at the behest of the local government, in 1964; and the Punan Batu have been "trickling" into it ever since. A small nucleus of these people have settled permanently, have adopted Islam, and no longer consider themselves Punan. Rather, they say that they are now Orang Bulungan—the local ethnic variant of coastal Malay culture. Others in the village, however, divide their time in varying degrees between the forest and the village. As such, there are families who are alternately counted as "settled" Punan Sajau and "nomadic" Punan Batu.

This entire aggregate of groups moved into the Sajau area about forty years ago from its former territory in the Berau Regency. At the present day, a culturally and linguistically similar nomadic people may be found around the upper Birang River—a tributary of the Berau River. This group, however, is referred to as Basap and not Punan.†

Punan Berun, Punan Benyawung

The Punan Berun and the Punan Benyawung are closely related groups living at the headwaters of two small tributaries of the Kayan River and its middle reaches, in the Peso district of the Bulungan Regency. They are small groups;

---

*The largest internal administrative unit in Indonesia is the *propinsi,* or province. Each province is divided into several *kabupaten,* or regencies; each regency is further divided into *kecamatan,* or districts.

†There are several distinct, unrelated groups called Basap dispersed throughout the coastal areas of eastern Kalimantan. In addition to the Basap of the upper Birang, there is one other nomadic group of this name living in the coastal forests of the Mangkalihat Peninsula, in the districts of Talisayan and Sangkulirang. These people are apparently unrelated to the nomadic Birang River group. All of the other Basap peoples I am aware of are sedentary agricultural groups.

the Punan Berun numbering (in 1980) 105 people and the Punan Benyawung approximately 50. At the time of my fieldwork these people had been nominally settled for three years. Most families were already engaged in agriculture; others were still spending most of their time in the forest. Each of these groups is located in close proximity to a village of the sedentary, agricultural Kayan Malaran people, the Punan Berun being near the village of Long Telenjau, the Punan Benyawung near the village of Long Naha Ayah. All of these groups—Punan Berun, Punan Benyawung, and Kayan Malaran—are relatively recent migrants to the Peso area, having come to their present locations some forty years ago from farther up the Kayan River. Prior to this migration and regrouping downriver, the Punan Berun and the Punan Benyawung were both parts of a larger group then known as the Punan Bahau.

Punan of the Tubu and Malinau Rivers

This is the largest congeries of Punan groups in Kalimantan. Though widely dispersed, this aggregate is centered mainly around the headwaters and tributaries of the Tubu River in the Malinau district of the Bulungan Regency. Local groups have their own specific names of reference, each group being known by the name of a stream or tributary with which it traditionally was associated, e.g., Punan Menabur Besar, Punan Menabur Kecil, Punan Pangin, Punan Bayang, Punan Lihi. These are residential groupings and not discrete units; all are united by webs of kinship and marriage, and all are characterized by an ever-changing composition.

Punan of the Tubu have all been nominally settled for a generation or more, but individuals and whole families continue to enter the forest for weeks at a time. As a result of major relocation programs conducted within the last five years by the local government, about half of the Tubu Punan, along with all of the sedentary, agricultural Tebilun people, have been induced to move out of the Tubu River and to settle in more accessible locations. Most of these people are now living in a large, government-built, government-run village of roughly 1,000 inhabitants located about fifteen minutes by boat from the town of Malinau. There are still, however, five Punan villages at the Tubu, three of these being near the headwaters and two at tributaries known respectively as Rian and Kalun.

Culturally and linguistically related to the Punan of the Tubu are several groups living at the upper reaches of the nearby Malinau River. Like the Tubu Punan, the Punan of the Malinau have been nominally settled for about thirty years but continue to leave their villages—individually and in family groupings—for weeks at a time in the forest. These Malinau River Punan are almost invariably found living in close proximity to a settled people known as the Merap, in much the same manner as Punan of the Tubu lived near the Tebilun prior to their recent relocation. Whereas Punan of the Malinau may be seen as an ethnic extension of the Tubu Punan, the Merap are similarly related to the Tebilun. All of these peoples together form a sort of areal culture complex.

Small segments of this Tubu-Malinau aggregate of Punan are also to be found at scattered locations in the neighboring Mentarang district. I did not, however, visit these segments.

There is also one small group of roughly six households who reside in the previously mentioned Peso district, living some thirty minutes by boat from Long Leju, a village of the Kenyah Uma Kulit people. Although aware of having migrated from the Tubu, this group had no firm idea of how long they had been living in their present location.

Punan Oho

The Punan Oho are a small group of eight households living at the headwaters of the Oho River in a village called Long Top, in the Kayan Hulu district of the Bulungan Regency. This group was previously more numerous; some of its members have moved southwards to the upper Mahakam area while others have returned to the group's ancestral home in Sarawak.

Kayan Hulu, along with the adjacent district of Kayan Hilir, makes up an area known in Borneo as the Apo Kayan. In this mountainous region is the source of the long, meandering Kayan River. Despite the relative remoteness and inaccessibility of the area, the Punan Oho were settled during the Dutch colonial period. They have long since become full-fledged agriculturalists whose well-tended gardens and swiddens compare favorably with those of the longhouse Kenyah people from such nearby villages as Long Lebusan, Mahak, and Long Nawang.

Punan Kelai

The Punan Kelai are a widely dispersed group of unknown numbers scattered throughout the upper reaches and tributaries of the Kelai River, in the Kelai district of the Berau Regency. Like the previously mentioned Punan Berun, Punan Benyawung, and Punan groups of the Tubu and Malinau area, the Punan Kelai are what might best be described as sporadically settled. A common feature of their small, scattered villages throughout the Kelai is empty dwellings whose owners are off in the forest.

A similarly dispersed group, related culturally and linguistically to the Punan Kelai, live to the north at the upper reaches of the Segah River, in the

Segah district of the Berau Regency. As might be expected, they are called the Punan Segah. Not having visited this group, my knowledge of these people derives from information furnished by government officials, Malay and Arab traders, and the Punan Kelai. Both the Punan Kelai and the Punan Segah have traditionally tended to live in close proximity to villages of a sedentary, agricultural people known as the Segai.

Punan Lisum, Punan Beketan

These are two culturally and linguistically similar groups dispersed throughout the upper Belayan River area, in the Tabang district of the Kutai Regency. Both groups have been settled and agricultural for about two generations. The Punan Lisum have been centered mainly at the upper reaches of the Belinau River; the Punan Beketan are found chiefly along the Tuboq. These small rivers are tributaries of the Belayan, which is itself an affluent of the Mahakam.

Both of these groups have been the objects of concerted relocation efforts exerted by the provincial government. As a result, about three-fourths of the Punan Lisum in 1981 had moved out of the Belinau River and had resettled in a large, government-built village some twenty minutes by boat from the town of Tabang. In this new village called Sungai Lunuk, the Punan Lisum lived interspersed among Kenyahs from East Kalimantan, Kahayans from Central Kalimantan, Banjars from South Kalimantan, and Orang Kutai—the local variety of what are known generally as coastal Malays. At the time of my fieldwork, one Punan Lisum village remained at the Belinau; and most of the Punan Beketan were still at the Tuboq, few having chosen to relocate.

It can perhaps be said that relocation is by no means a new phenomenon for these groups. Both the Punan Lisum and Punan Beketan are relatively recent migrants to the Belayan area, having come originally from contiguous localities in Sarawak, adjacent to the Apo Kayan. As such, not only are the languages of the two groups similar, they both display a marked linguistic affinity to the previously mentioned Punan Oho, as evidenced in wordlists collected from all three groups.

These Punan did not, however, migrate alone. Rather, they were part of a general movement in the early years of this century that involved sedentary Kenyah people as well. Oral histories from Punan Lisum and Punan Beketan informants indicate that this mass departure from the Sarawak border area was due primarily to population pressures and depredations by Ibans. Both Punan groups claim to have segments remaining in Sarawak—families that had planned to migrate, but subsequently opted to remain behind when peace was established around 1920.

Punan Murung

All of the Punan groups listed above are located within the province of East Kalimantan. The Punan Murung, however, are found within the northernmost district of Central Kalimantan province.

The Punan Murung derive their name from the term used locally to refer to the Barito River at its uppermost reaches. This group maintains that its traditional territory in former times was the mountainous, heavily forested area between the headwaters of the Barito and the upper reaches of the Mahakam. They have been settled since the 1930s, however, and are presently dispersed throughout the three final villages of the Barito River—Tumbang Kramu, Tumbang Tujang, and Tumbang Tupus—in the Sumber Barito district of the Barito Utara Regency. The Punan share these settlements with members of other ethnic groups who, by their own accounts, have always been sedentary agriculturists. At Tumbang Kramu the Punan live intermixed with Ot Danum; upriver at Tumbang Tujang they are found with roughly equal numbers of Ot Danum and Siang, and finally at Tumbang Tupus they live chiefly with Siang.

In 1981 there were ten households nominally resident at Tumbang Kramu, twenty-seven at Tumbang Tujang, and fourteen at Tumbang Tupus. It is nearly impossible to say with any certainty, however, exactly how many Punan these households represent. This ambiguity arises out of the fact that it is nearly impossible to ascertain exactly what constitutes a Punan in these villages at the present date. Intermarriage and assimilation have occurred to such an extent that whatever "ethnic boundaries" might have existed between these groups in the past have all but broken down. This situation is displayed most dramatically at Tumbang Tupus, where virtually everyone is multilingual in Siang, Punan Murung, and Ot Danum and where the same individuals alternately refer to themselves as Siang and Punan.

The Punan Murung are, to the best of my knowledge, the only Punan group in Central Kalimantan. They are not the only group of recently nomadic people; they are, however, the only such group known as Punan.

Westward of the Punan Murung, but at approximately the same general latitude, is a formerly nomadic group known as the Kareho. They are found on the Busang, a small river flowing into the Joloi, which in turn joins the Barito River at a point near the Ot Danum village of Muara Joloi. These people were formerly known as the Penyabung—a name they presently reject as pejorative. This group was the subject of three colorful and rather lurid chapters of a popular travel account that appeared more than five decades ago, by "adventurer" Eugene Wright (1928:220-44). They were described then as living in villages; and the Kareho themselves say that they ceased to be nomadic about sixty years ago.

They are presently living in two villages along the Busang, called Parahau and Jojang Parit respectively. I did not enter the Busang or visit these villages; their names were supplied by several Kareho I met at Muara Joloi.

Other Punan of Kalimantan

There are various other groups of Punan in Kalimantan in addition to those I was able to study. Most of these are located within the province of East Kalimantan, and principally in the Bulungan Regency (cf. Whittier, 1974; Appell, 1982), although a few small groups are reported to be present along the Mahakam River in the Kutai Regency as well (Bernard Sellato, personal communication). In the province of West Kalimantan, where I did not conduct research, Victor King (1974) notes the presence of some settled Punan in several small villages at the upper reaches of the Kapuas River.

The ethnographic overview that follows, let me say again, derives solely from my observations among the groups that I visited.

Nomenclature

As has been noted, the term Punan is applied not only to present and recent hunters and gatherers, but also to some sedentary agricultural peoples who have no traditions of prior nomadism. Moreover, there are several groups of present and former nomads who are known by names other than Punan.

The term Punan seems originally to have been an exonym—a name by which a group is referred to by other peoples. It was my observation that the word Punan was far more commonly a term of reference applied to nomads by sedentary peoples than an actual label of identity for the nomads themselves The latter will, on occasion, refer to themselves as Punan, but they are usually more prone to speak of themselves using some local lexeme meaning "us." In either case, Punan is rarely a meaningful ethnic name in the minds of peoples so termed. This is particularly true of such groups as the Punan Lisum, who in former times often encountered other groups called Punan who came from other areas, spoke different languages, observed different customs, and with whom the Punan Lisum had no feelings of kinship or commonality. Punan Lisum often cite the Punan Kelai as an example of these other types of Punan.

The precise meaning and derivation of the word Punan is unclear. Harrisson (1949) maintained that in several of the Dayak languages with which he was familiar, *punan* is synonymous with the Malay word *hulu*, meaning "upriver" or "headwaters of a river." When I myself asked the various sedentary agricultural peoples I met to relate their own definitions of Punan, the responses included "people who live up at the source of the river," "people who live deep within the forest," "people always moving from place to place," and "people who do not plant gardens and swiddens and must hunt for their food." Kenyah at Long Nawang and Ot Danum at Muara Joloi reported that in each of their languages, *punan* is a verb meaning "to assemble, pile up, or gather things together." What seems to emerge from these various definitions is the probability that, for native peoples of Kalimantan, the use of the word Punan to designate groups of people involves more a description of *locational and behavioral characteristics* than assumptions of ethnic origin.

Let us note finally that for any one group, the term Punan invariably is used in conjunction with some sort of toponym denoting the name of a river, tributary, or specific location at which the group is believed to reside. The Punan Berun are thus the Punan *of* the Berun River, the Punan Benyawung are the Punan *of* the Benyawung, and so on. These are largely terms of identification, used by sedentary people to refer to a specific Punan group, and by one Punan group to refer to another. A term such as this is rarely a label of identity by which people refer to themselves. A Punan of the Berun River, for example, is most unlikely to call himself a Punan Berun; he might, however, speak of Punan of the Kelai River as Punan Kelai.

Inasmuch as these groups are nomadic, or were nomadic until recently, these names are often ephemeral. Groups lose their old names and have new ones bestowed upon them as they move from one place to another. There are Punan groups of the Upper Tubu River that are each known by two or three variant names, depending upon where they happened to be situated when the various names were imposed. There are other groups from the Tubu who were known alternately by the names of their villages and by the names of the tributaries where the villages were located.

Finally, there are groups that have migrated to their present areas from elsewhere, that are now called by names different from those they had a generation or two ago. Today's Punan Berun and Punan Benyawung, for example, were yesterday's Punan Bahau.

It became evident rather early on in my fieldwork that trying to ascertain the "real names" of Punan groups was a matter far more important to me than it was to the Punan themselves.

Racial Affinities

Elsewhere in Southeast Asia, there are certain small, putatively-aboriginal groups that clearly appear to be racially distinct from the larger populations that surround them. Such is the case with the Semang of the Malay Peninsula and the Aeta of the Philippines. Both of these are Negrito peoples, characterized by black skin color, tightly spiraled or frizzy hair, and short stature. As such they form what are more or less genetic isolates, differing physically from their generalized Malay-type neighbors.

All of the Punan groups with which I am familiar are racially identical to the surrounding sedentary agricultural Dayak peoples. Punan share with Dayaks generally the basic proto-Malay somatological characteristics of medium stature, prominent muscularity, and Mongoloid facial features and hair form. In short, there would appear to be no physical evidence to suggest that the Punan are essentially distinct and apart from Dayak peoples in general, or that Punan and sedentary agricultural people derive from different origins.

Linguistic Affinities

In many instances throughout Borneo, linguistic evidence strongly suggests that a certain ethnic label does in fact reflect a uniform, discrete ethnic group. Such is the case, for example, with the ethnic category Iban. Although widely dispersed throughout Sarawak, the various Iban subgroups share a common, relatively homogeneous language in which internal variation is minimal (LeBar, 1972:180-81). The term Kayan similarly reflects a group whose scattered segments "everywhere speak closely related dialects" (ibid.:169). Each of these peoples is moreover characterized by both a high degree of cultural uniformity and a strong sense of ethnic identity.

The various groups known as Punan, however, do not share a single, common language. There is no general Punan language spoken overall by the peoples so termed. Instead, the linguistic evidence suggests the presence of several language clusters into which the various Punan peoples I studied may be classed. Linguistic similarity is evident within each cluster; marked divergence is present between clusters.

One such language cluster is formed by the Punan Batu, Punan Binai, and Punan Sajau of the Tanjung Palas district, along with a historically related group of hunters and gatherers called Basap, who live to the south in the Gunung Tabor district. The three Punan groups share one common language; the Basap speak a closely related dialect.

Another cluster of closely related dialects is evident among the Punan groups of the Malinau and Tubu River area, Punan of the Mentarang River as well as the migrant Punan group living near Long Leju in the Peso district.

As one would expect, the historically related Punan Berun and Punan Benyawung speak the same language. A comparison of wordlists suggests an affinity between this language and that of the Punan Kelai.

A similar case is presented by the Punan Lisum and Punan Beketan, whose closely similar languages show a marked affinity with that spoken by the Punan Oho of the Apo Kayan. Although a substantial geographic distance now separates the two former groups from the latter, all three peoples claim to have originated in the same general area in Sarawak.

We are left finally with the Punan Murung of the upper Barito, whose language displays no close affinity with any of the above-mentioned clusters.

Between the various language clusters, the situation is one of divergence. The languages within one cluster are mutually unintelligible with those of another. An interesting example of this may be seen in the Peso district, where we have the Punan Berun and Punan Benyawung on the one hand, and the Punan near Long Leju on the other. As has been noted, both of these types of Punan migrated to this area from elsewhere, the former from the west and the latter from the north. Although they now live within a few miles of each other in the same district, the two peoples do not interact. On the rare occasions in which Punan Berun-Benyawung encounter Punan from Long Leju, they are forced to use the Kayan language as a medium of communication, as neither people understands the other's language.

In this same regard, I was told by two Punan informants from the Tubu River of an incident that occurred as the two were traveling once through the upper Mahakam. It seems they happened upon some Punan of a type they had never encountered before. My informants were not certain who these Punan were, or where they had come from. They related to me, in somewhat humorous detail, their difficulties in trying to communicate with these people. They said that they and the "other" Punan were totally unable to make themselves understood in either their respective languages or in any native language the two parties were familiar with. They finally had recourse to Malay.

There is another point to be raised apropos of language. Regardless of the diversity evident among the different language clusters of the Punan groups that I studied, they are all simply variants of Borneo languages generally. The Punan do not form any sort of linguistic isolate; they do not speak languages unrelated to those spoken by sedentary agricultural peoples. Rather, the Punan groups that I studied speak Austronesian languages similar to those spoken by other native peoples of Borneo.

Moreover, it would appear that certain Punan languages are closely related to those of certain sedentary agriculturists. The Punan Kelai, for example, insisted that their language was "very close" to that of the Segai. Punan Lisum told me over and over again that the language they speak is similar and mutually intelligible with that of a Kenyah group called the Lepo Timai.

If any one conclusion can be drawn from the examination of Punan linguistic affinities, it is simply that linguistic evidence does not support the assumption that the "Punan" comprise a single, uniform people who are ethnically distinct from sedentary agriculturists.

Traditional Patterns of Residence

Within the last decade, many erstwhile nomadic groups in Kalimantan have, to greater or lesser degrees, chosen to settle into fixed villages. Some groups have done this at their own initiative, others as the result of concerted government efforts. The Punan Berun and Punan Benyawung are notable examples of recently settled peoples.

Elsewhere, certain groups that already were settled have been induced to move downriver and resettle in less remote locales. Examples of this can be seen most dramatically in the Malinau district of East Kalimantan, where Punan of the Tubu—along with their sedentary neighbors, the Tebilun—have been the objects of major relocation programs by the Department of Internal Resettlement, known by its acronym RESPEN.

Finally there are such groups as the Punan Murung and the Punan Oho, for whom the process of settlement into fixed villages began as far back as Dutch colonial times.

As such, any general description of traditional patterns of residence for most of the groups I visited must be based largely upon the recollections of older informants. Fortunately, however, there are still some presently nomadic Punan, for whom "historical reconstruction" is unnecessary. These are the Punan Batu and Punan Binai of the Tanjung Palas district, who continue to roam through the heavily forested upper reaches and tributaries of the Sajau River. Whereas their traditional residence pattern persists and still can be observed, we shall begin our discussion with these groups.

The Punan Batu rarely live together in one place as a single group. This, by extension, is also true of the Punan Binai (as well as the related Basap group to the south). The usual pattern of residence involves a small grouping of two or three nuclear families, related by blood or marriage, living together in a temporary encampment in the forest by a stream at the headwaters of a river. Under normal circumstances, each of these nuclear families may have as many as three coresident dependents—aged widows, visitors from another camp, and the like.

Each of these encampments is usually no more than an hour's walk (for Punan, not anthropologists) from at least one other similar encampment of two or three households. Quite often, several such local groups may be found within the radius of a day's walk from any single encampment. Moreover, as these encampments invariably are made near a stream, one is often able to encounter as many as three or four local groups by simply following the snaking course of one small tributary.

These local groups are by nature highly unstable units, subject to almost constant changes in personnel as individuals or whole families break away from one encampment to join another grouping some distance away. People leave their encampments for a variety of reasons, perhaps the most common being quarrels and disputes. The notion that there might be more game, fruit, or jungle produce in another part of the forest is also a frequent and effective motive to decamp and move elsewhere. Marriages and divorces are similarly compelling devices for sending people moving from one local group to another.

Whatever their reasons for moving and wherever they decide to go, it is reasonably certain that the newly decamped individual or family will keep within the loosely demarcated territory that the group as a whole considers to be its home range. It is within this vaguely bounded home range that the mobile individual or family can expect to encounter other members of the scattered group with whom they can encamp. There is a quite interesting phenomenon associated with this type of residence pattern, namely the use of various signs and markers to facilitate contact, relate messages, and spread news among the widely dispersed nomadic households. Within any one Punan band, there are always a number of generally understood signs, each imbued with its own meaning. All along the trails within a band's home range, and at various places recognized as landmarks by that group, one may see such things as a lone strip of rattan hanging from a branch, a stick laid horizontally across two low-hanging vines, a broken branch placed across the trail at a certain angle, or a piece of bark with several notches carved into its edge, put in a "conspicuous" place. I employ the word conspicuous with a certain amount of irony, as all of these signs, and others, were vastly more noticeable to Punan than they were to me. Nonetheless, Punan always watch for these markers while on the march through the forest, and they rarely are at a loss for knowing what they mean.

Let us say, for example, that two Punan Batu men are in the process of planning to meet at a certain spot in the forest ten days hence. Each cuts a strip of rattan and knots it ten times. Each then ties his knotted strip of rattan around his waist, whereupon the two men part and go their separate ways. Thereafter, as each new days dawns, each of the two men—now separated by miles of jungle—unties one of the knots in his strip of rattan. The process continues as the days pass until each man has arrived at the tenth knot in his strip of rattan, indicating that the meeting day has arrived. If one man arrives at the designated spot and finds that the other man is absent, he will immediately look about for some sign placed there by the missing man, indicating why he cannot make the meeting, what he is doing instead, and where he is doing it. There might be a broken branch, arranged in such a way as to signify that the man is ill or injured. Or perhaps there is a small stick, roughly carved into a point at one end, that indicates the man is hunting.

There might even be another strip of rattan displaying several knots, thus designating the number of days hence in which the missing man expects to return.

Signs and markers are numerous all along the trails that crisscross the group's home range. There are signs that point the way toward places where game is abundant, or where fruit is plentiful. Other signs lead people to honey. There are also signs that point away from areas that someone has recently surveyed and found lacking in game, fruit, and jungle products.

On one occasion while among the Punan Batu, I arrived at an empty lean-to, deep within the forest. The family that owned it was away gathering jungle products in another part of the group's territory. My two Punan Batu guides and I rested in the lean-to for a moment, whereupon I dug into my pack, extracted camera and film, and proceeded to photograph the lean-to from several different angles, much to the amusement of my guides. Moments later as we were preparing to leave, one of the men picked up the empty green and white cardboard box in which my film had been packaged, and placed it on the end of one of the lean-to's support-posts, to tell others in the band of the circumstances under which the hut was visited, and whom it was visited by.

This type of dispersed residence pattern also characterized the Punan Murung and the Punan Kelai in former times, as well as the Punan Berun and Punan Benyawung until recently. The latter three groups, however, claim to have preferred somewhat larger encampments of anywhere from five to ten households. The Punan Murung are unable to recall the size of their local groups in the past.

However, such groups a the Punan Oho, Punan Lisum, Punan Beketan, and the Punan of the Tubu and Malinau rivers do not recall ever having lived like this. Members of these groups were in fact surprised and amused at my descriptions of the Punan Batu. These peoples maintain that in the days when they were still nomadic they lived in large base camps that accommodated the entire group. Individuals and entire households, it is said, fanned out from the base camp—in different directions and at staggered times—to hunt and gather for periods of up to a week. Punan of the Tubu now say that their base camps tended to remain fixed in one spot for anywhere from three to five years; Malinau River Punan insist that theirs were often stationary for as long as ten years.

For all of these groups, nonetheless, this pattern may not have differed greatly *in effect* from that noted previously among the Punan Batu and Punan Binai, as I was able to infer from their recollections that these base camps were usually little more than storage places for rattan, resin, and other forest products. It seems that only a few people were actually to be found there at most times, the majority of the group being dispersed through the forest in several local group encampments.

I have used the term home range to refer to the traditional territory within which a Punan group has moved and encamped. It is time to examine the precise nature of a group's home range by drawing attention to its two most significant characteristics. Respectively, these two characteristics show *what* essentially the various home ranges have been and *where* they have been located.

Stated simply, the traditional home ranges of Punan groups have invariably been tracts of *primary forest.* A primary forest area is either one that has never been cleared for cultivation, or a previously cultivated area left fallow for so long that the resulting forest has returned to full growth. In either case, the area is one in which a wide array of different species of botanical life has grown to maturity. A primary forest topography is the first characteristic of a Punan group's traditional home range.

While all Punan groups traditionally have lived within tracts of primary forest, it is not conversely the case that all tracts of primary forest have had Punan groups living within them. Vast expanses of primary forest exist throughout Kalimantan wherein there are no Punan, or anyone else for that matter. Rather, each group known as Punan has tended to confine itself to a tract of primary forest *adjacent and contiguous to an area occupied by a specific sedentary agricultural people.* In actual terms, this has usually entailed a Punan group living at the headwaters and tributaries of a river that is occupied—in its lower reaches—by a specific sedentary people with whom the Punan group is affiliated. This group and this sedentary people thus share the same drainage area, in which the former are hunting and gathering upriver and the latter are living in villages downriver. This relative proximity to a specific sedentary agricultural people is the second characteristic of a Punan group's traditional home range.

The actual boundaries of such a home range have had relatively little to do with topography. The territory that a Punan group traditionally has considered its own has not been enclosed by such features as mountain ranges, valleys, or even rivers. The boundaries have instead been essentially sociological in nature.

The dispersed households of a Punan group have ranged about in an area of primary forest adjacent to an area occupied by a specific sedentary people with whom this group is culturally affiliated, and with whom it is involved in a symbiotic trading relationship. Every member of the Punan group has had in his mind a cognitive map of the larger region around him, showing an area belonging to *orang macam kita*—"people of our kind," which grades somewhat vaguely and indefinitely into surrounding areas occupied by *orang macam lain*—"people of other kinds."

Those of the first category, "people of our kind," have included the Punan group and the specific sedentary people with whom this group is economically interdependent, and with whom it shares similarities in customs, historical traditions, and sometimes language as well. Those belonging to the second category, "people of other kinds," are culturally and historically different; the members of the Punan group have perceived them as being *jauh* or "distant"—distant culturally as well as geographically.

As such, in its largest sense, the group's home range has been conceived of as being the maximal spatial area claimed (and in former times, defended) by both the group and its affiliated sedentary neighbors. Individual families moving about in the forest have held in mind the ultimate constraint of not wanting to stray too far from "our kind" of people and too close to the various "other kinds" of people. It is this mental constraint that above all else has provided the actual boundaries of a group's home range in the traditional pattern of residence—boundaries every bit as real and far more effective than topographical markers.

The traditional conception, however, of just where it is exactly that the territory belonging to "our kind" ends and that belonging to "other kinds" begins usually has been rather vague. Indeed, in former times it was largely putative. Disputes over territory and encroachment by "other kinds" of people were among the major causes of intergroup warfare, not only between a Punan group and some other different sedentary people, but between that group and some other different Punan group as well.

It has been mentioned that many Punan groups recently either have moved into fixed villages or have been induced to relocate their old villages into less remote locales. Many of these peoples, however, are still only nominally or sporadically settled, in that whole families frequently leave their villages to hunt and gather forest products in the jungle for days and weeks at a time. It is noteworthy that when they do so, these families continue to return almost exclusively to the traditional home range of their particular group.

We have thus been able to see that the two most salient characteristics of a Punan group's traditional home range have been that it is primary forest and that it is a tract of primary forest adjacent to an area occupied by an affiliated sedentary agricultural people. This usually has entailed a situation in which a particular Punan group has lived at the headwaters and tributaries of a river occupied in its lower reaches by the affiliated sedentary people.

For the present-day Punan Berun and Punan Benyawung, both formerly the Punan Bahau, that affiliated sedentary people are the Kayan Malaran. For Punan of the Tubu, the affiliated people are the Tebilun; for Punan of the Malinau, the Merap. A similar pattern prevails for the Punan Kelai, for whom the affiliated sedentary people are the Segai. For the Punan Lisum and Punan Beketan, "our kind" of people included the Kenyah Lepo Timai. For the Punan Oho it has been the Kenyah Lepo Tau. And for the Punan Murung, the affiliated sedentary people have been Siang and Ot Danum groups of the upper Barito.

The only exception to this general pattern in the groups that I studied is that presented by the currently nomadic Punan Batu-Punan Binai. Unlike the other Punan groups, these people are not found in the island's interior, but rather at the coast. Their home range at the headwaters of the Sajau River displays the first characteristic of being primary forest, but not the second. These people, along with a related group called Basap immediately to the south and another group of that name on the Mangkalihat Peninsula, are highly specialized nomads of the coastal forests of East Kalimantan. As such, they do not interact with Dayak peoples of the interior, but rather with coastal Malays. As a result of this unusual interaction, these peoples are different from interior Punan groups in some other ways as well, which we shall examine in detail in chapter 3.

Subsistence Technology

Like hunters and gatherers elsewhere in the world, Punan groups of Kalimantan have made use of a wide range of animal resources available to them. Punan share with Dayaks generally an intense fondness for wild pigs, *babi hutan,* this being by far *the* food of preference among every Punan group of which I am aware. In addition, two species of large wild deer, called *payau* and *rusa,* are greatly favored, as is, to a lesser extent, the *kancil* or mouse deer. Punan will also eat such animals as monkeys, snakes, and the *bruang* or Malay bear, but they are likely to obtain this sort of game by happening upon it inadvertently rather than by setting out to hunt it deliberately.

As among sedentary peoples, the primary hunting weapon of all Punan groups is the *sumpit* or blowpipe—a long ironwood shaft of anywhere from six to eight feet in length (varying according to region), with a quarter inch-wide hole bored through it, and with an iron blade mounted bayonet-fashion to the business end. As an example of primitive manufacture and craftsmanship, the *sumpit* is remarkable. To begin with, the wood is taken from one or another variety of hardwood trees—usually *kayu besi* or *kayu ulin*—and subjected to rough, preliminary carving to a size and shape manageable for further working. A high platform is then utilized, or constructed if need be, upon which the maker of the blowpipe stands. A hole is made in the floor of the platform, through which the wood to be worked is passed so that it stands upright. The blowpipe maker uses a long narrow iron bore to make the hole through the length of the wood. He does this by repeatedly thrusting the bore deeper and deeper into the wood, stopping occasionally to pour water down the hole to float up the chips. When he has bored about halfway through the wood, the maker turns the wood upside down and bores his hole from the other end until it, at last, runs through the entire length of the wood. Even more remarkable, knowing that the blowpipe will bend downward slightly when in use, the worker compensates for this by making a slight upward rise in the middle of the shaft. Having completed the hole successfully, he finishes the job by carving and sanding the outside of the blowpipe until it is perfectly round and smooth. A razor-sharp iron blade lashed to the firing end with rattan completes the procedure, so that the blowpipe can double as a spear.

The *sumpit* is used, of course, in conjunction with poisoned darts. These most often are made entirely of wood, although one group was seen making dart tips from metal retrieved from discarded tin cans. The manufacture of poison for the darts varies somewhat from one region to another. Most often extracted from certain types of vines or from the leaves and roots of certain plants, the poison is fast-acting and deadly. All of the Punan groups I encountered informed me that a dart dipped in poison remains lethal for a year at the very least.

In addition to their blowpipes, Punan make liberal use of spears. These are iron blades lashed with rattan to the ends of crudely carved sticks. Generally speaking, Punan will use spears, rather than blowpipes, when they are hunting with the aid of dogs.

As with the sedentary peoples, all Punan groups employ dogs when hunting wild pigs. The dogs track the pig through the woods and surround it until the hunter arrives to dispatch it with his spear. Five dogs usually are considered to be the optimum number for a successful hunt; three dogs are the minimum. Dogs are used for hunting—they are neither kept as pets nor resorted to as food.

Despite the fact that dogs raised and kept by Punan groups are of identical breed to those kept by Dayaks generally, and despite furthermore their identically gaunt, mangy, and flea-bitten appearance, the dogs of Punan groups are esteemed throughout eastern and central Kalimantan as being far superior to others in their ability to track and surround game. Not only do sedentary peoples wish to obtain dogs from Punan for their own hunting needs, they will often hold in noticeably higher regard any of their own dogs that are descended—however many generations ago—from a dog given to them by the nearby Punan group.

Blowpipes, spears, and dogs make up the essential inventory of equipment used for hunting by Punan groups. The bow and arrow are unknown throughout Borneo generally, and the use of firearms is prohibited by the Indonesian government.

Like all of the sedentary, agricultural, native peoples of Borneo, Punan groups live near water. Traditionally, they have roamed and encamped at the headwaters and tributaries of the same rivers that sedentary people inhabit farther downstream. The currently nomadic Punan Batu and Punan Binai will always encamp near a stream, no matter how small. As such, one need not spend more than a few days among any Punan group to know that *in terms of subsistence,* their way of life has involved a riverine adaptation as much as a forest adaptation. Punan groups are thus as skillful at fishing as they are at hunting.

Fish are obtained by a variety of methods, the most common being the use of nets. Punan are agile users of cast nets, and they deploy fixed nets to good advantage as well. Some Punan groups, such as those of the upper Barito area, are clever builders of dams and weirs. Others make use of various plant poisons, which they pour into small streams and rivers to stupify the fish. These poisons, or *tuba* as they are called, are generally quite effective. Moments after they are poured into the headwaters of a stream, fish can be seen swimming with difficulty or simply floating listlessly to the top, at which point they can be taken with spears, nets, baskets, or even by hand. This sort of fishing generally takes the form of a major communal operation, involving the entire group or village. All of these techniques—the use of cast nets, fixed nets, dams, weirs, and plant poisons—are commonly employed by sedentary agricultural peoples as well.

Food gathering continues to supplement the produce of hunting and fishing in the diets of still nomadic Punan. Punan Batu and Punan Binai avail themselves of the wide variety of wild fruits to be found in their home range, *durian* and *rambutan* especially. They utilize also a type of ferm called *paku*; and they are also quite adept at gathering wild honey, of which they are especially fond.

The use of wild sago, however, is rapidly falling into decline. Many of the Punan Batu and Punan Binai are presently more prone to practice a halfhearted and tenuous form of horticulture in poorly tended, widely scattered gardens than go to the trouble of extracting sago and preparing it for consumption. Some members of these groups also receive rice from settled relatives among the Punan Sajau.

Among the other Punan groups of my acquaintance, wild sago is rarely if ever resorted to at all. I observed its use only among Punan of the upper Tubu. Otherwise, even such seminomadic peoples as the Punan Kelai and the Punan Berun are much more likely to take quantities of their own swidden-grown rice with them when they leave their villages for days or weeks in the forest. A family preparing to enter the forest simply fill a basket or two with as much rice as they anticipate they will need.

The various settled Punan groups do, however, continue to supplement their diets by gathering wild fruits and honey. Inasmuch as these people now engage in agriculture, food gathering is no longer strictly necessary. Their gardens and swiddens are generally comparable in productivity to those of their sedentary neighbors. Wild fruits and wild honey are nonetheless still gathered, as settled Punan remain fond of these foods.

Like the sedentary peoples, all of the Punan groups that I studied have had food storage and preservation as part of their subsistence technologies. Even the most nomadic Punan preserve small quantities of food—often for months at a time—to tide themselves over during periods of bad hunting. Even if such times rarely occur, nomadic Punan will preserve foodstuff out of nothing more than a sensible aversion to wasting food.

Punan preserve fish in the same manner practiced throughout Kalimantan, namely by salting it and drying it in the sun. This most often is done with the immense quantities of fish obtained from those occasions in which *tuba* poison has been used. Rendered pig fat, or *minyak babi* as it is called, is also kept for months on end. It generally is stored in large ceramic jars, more often than not thickened with a few well-cooked pieces of meat and gristle. It is most commonly poured directly over cooked rice and eaten in the absence of fresh meat. Finally, surplus meat from a large deer is preserved by smoking it for several hours over an open fire.

We have noted that all Punan groups, like sedentary agriculturists, raise and keep dogs for hunting. This has been the only domesticated animal among nomadic Punan. Settled Punan, however, have adopted the sedentary peoples' custom of keeping chickens and, occasionally, pigs.

Before turning from the topic of subsistence, let me state explicitly a point that the reader has perhaps already begun to appreciate. None of the subsistence techniques noted in the preceding discussion—techniques traditionally associated in our minds with Punan—are peculiar to Punan alone. The subsistence activities and techniques that Punan have practiced are common among sedentary peoples as well. Blowpipes, spears, and dogs make up the inventory of equipment used for hunting not only by Punan but by every sedentary people of which I am aware. Sedentary peoples are no less skillful at using this equipment than Punan, nor are their occasional hunting forays noticeably less successful. Sedentary peoples employ the same techniques to obtain fish as Punan employ, and they lose nothing in comparison to Punan in their ability to fish. Sedentary agriculturists are, moreover, similar to Punan in that they too supplement their diets by gathering wild fruit and honey, and many of these peoples likewise have made use of wild sago, if only as a starch food of last resort during periods of bad harvests (cf. LeBar, 1972:169,195; Peranio, 1972:164).

There is, as such, no *qualitative* difference between the subsistence technology of Punan groups and that of sedentary agricultural peoples. Stated simply: with regard to subsistence, Punan groups do nothing that is not done by sedentary people as well. The difference is one of emphasis.

Housing and Material Technology

The dwellings of nomadic Punan are small and simple, constructed to be little more than shelters against the rain. The hut, or *pondok,* of a nomadic Punan family is fashioned with wooden sticks as supports, leaves for roofing, and split bamboo pieces or small sticks for flooring—all held together with strips of rattan. There are neither walls nor internal partitions. The roof slopes downward from the front to the back. These small, rectangularly-shaped *pondok*—more like lean-to's than huts—are built directly upon the ground with the bamboo or stick flooring no more than one or two inches above the soil. Dwellings of this type are fashioned not only by the still nomadic Punan Batu and Punan Binai, but also by settled Punan when they enter the forest to hunt and collect jungle products.

The village houses of settled Punan, constructed of wooden planks and set upon piles several feet off the ground, are not appreciably different from the usual sort of single family, Malay-style houses common among sedentary Dayaks of the present day. Exceptions are houses of Punan groups that are relatively newly settled. These groups, of which the Punan Berun and Punan Benyawung are notable examples, construct dwellings identical to the type that sedentary agricultural peoples build at their swiddens. These are square-shaped huts, much larger than forest *pondok,* with gabled thatch roofs that slope downward to the sides. They are fashioned on wooden piles and stand several feet above the ground; access is gained by use of a log with small notches carved in for toe holds. Such dwellings make the new settlements of these Punan groups look somewhat like transitional hybrids between forest encampments and full-fledged villages.

The household goods and personal possessions of nomadic Punan, past and present, have been few in number. This is what one would expect of highly mobile people who need to travel light. A spear, a *sumpit,* a bamboo container of wooden darts, a small gourd container for the dart heads, one or two *parang*—the all-purpose machetes used by Dayaks throughout Borneo—encased in wooden sheaths, a couple of cooking pots, perhaps a wok, several rattan baskets, and a couple of woven rattan mats make up the normal assemblage of articles found in a *pondok* inhabited by nomadic Punan.

While *parang* have been made by sedentary Dayaks and metal cooking pots derive ultimately from the Chinese, the other items mentioned above have been made by Punan groups themselves. While meager in number, these articles have displayed a prodigious amount of care and craftsmanship. Perhaps nowhere is this more obvious than in the rattan mats and baskets for which certain Punan groups have been famous throughout their respective regions. These mats and baskets are usually made by women, who expend inordinate time and energy in slicing the rattan into strips of proper size, dyeing portions of it black, and then plaiting it by hand into intricate geometric patterns. Punan Lisum women are noted as superb mat and basket makers, as are women of the Punan Aput, a group formerly of Sarawak and now resident in the Kayan Hilir district of East Kalimantan. The rattan work of these and other Punan groups compares favorably with analogous native handicraft elsewhere in the world, and it may one day form the basis of a profitable cottage industry. The precise methods by which Punan men make blowpipes have already been described.

The household goods and personal possessions of most settled Punan groups are generally more numerous and elaborate, consisting of all the factory-made, store-bought items common to present day Dayaks in general. These entail, in addition to those articles noted above, drinking glasses and dishware, as well as wristwatches, cassette players and shortwave radios, and occasionally outboard gasoline engines for boats, as many settled Punan families have long, narrow *prahu,* or canoes, of local manufacture.

Traditionally, the clothing of a Punan group in former times differed not in kind but rather in *amount* from that worn by the group's sedentary agricultural neighbors. Generally speaking, the members of a Punan group tended to look somewhat like "underdressed" versions of the sedentary people with whom they were affiliated.

The principal, and sometimes only article of clothing for most Punan groups was simply that which was the *basic* article of clothing for most of the sedentary peoples, namely the loincloth or *cawat.* I know of no Punan group that went about totally naked. Loincloths traditionally were made of bark cloth, or *kulit kayu,* but this material is rarely used in the present day. The Punan Berun and Punan Benyawung continue to wear loincloths, but these are fashioned from lengths of factory-made cloth received in trade from the sedentary Kayan Malaran. The still nomadic Punan Batu and Punan Binai on occasion still make loincloths of *kulit kayu,* but their normal clothing now consists largely of commercially made bathing trunks and T-shirts for men and full-length dresses—or bras and sarongs—for women. These articles of clothing are obtained in trade with coastal Malay and Buginese traders.

Items of personal adornment worn by a Punan group similarly have been abbreviated and simplified versions of those worn by nearby sedentary agriculturists. We find, for example, that the elongated earlobes, the wearing of earrings, and the profuse body tattooing that characterize Kenyahs of Sarawak and the Apo Kayan have all been emulated—in simplified form—by the Punan Oho, Punan Lisum, and Punan Beketan. The Punan Batu and Punan Binai, however, reside near the coast and display none of these features.

The clothing and adornment of settled Punan differ not one iota from that of Dayaks generally in Kalimantan today. Men wear trousers, button-down shirts, and pullover jerseys; women wear dresses or blouses and sarongs. Wristwatches are common, as are factory-made pieces of jewelry.

Economic Activity

The various Punan groups being described in this chapter share in common the fact that they are present or recent nomadic hunters and gatherers. All of these groups, either now or in the past, have met their subsistence needs by hunting wild game and by gathering wild sago, fruits, and honey. None of these groups, however, has been fully self-sufficient economically. Each and every Punan group with which I am familiar has been involved in some sort of regular, ongoing trade relationship with nonnomadic people.

It is through trade that Punan groups have received a small but crucial assortment of essential commodities, the most important of these being metal. Unlike the natives of highland New Guinea, many of whom use stone tools and weapons to the present day, Borneo peoples have relied on metal for centuries. Nomadic hunters and gatherers have been no exception. Punan groups have needed *parang*—the multipurpose iron machetes used by Dayaks throughout the island—to cut trees for wood, vines for dart poison, sago palms for food, rattan for lashing, and slain animals for meat. *Parang* are needed to cut fruit from trees, to clear underbrush from trails, and to slice rattan into strips for plaiting baskets and mats. The *parang* is the consummate tool for jungle life.

Punan groups, moreover, have needed knife blades for weapons in hunting and warfare. Knife blades are lashed with rattan to the firing end of blowpipes, and knife blades are lashed with rattan to the ends of sticks to make spears. To obtain knife blades and *parang,* Punan groups have engaged in trade.

As Punan groups have needed metal, so likewise have they required salt. It is generally the case that the diets of most of the interior peoples of Borneo are naturally low in salt. These peoples thus have had to supplement the low salt intake derived from their plant and animal foods with refined salt. Punan groups have provisioned themselves with salt in the same manner in which they have obtained metal implements—through trade.

In addition to these essential commodities, Punan groups have traded to obtain tobacco, of which, like sedentary Dayaks, they are inordinately fond. They have traded also for cloth and clothing, and for such items of adornment as necklaces and bracelets made of stone or glass beads, metal earrings, and tattooing needles—depending upon the particular group. Some groups have traded to obtain large ceramic jars and brass gongs, important status items held in high regard by native peoples throughout the island.

On the eve of my visit to the Punan Oho of the Apo Kayan area, I received information about this group from Kenyah Lepo Tau people at the village of Long Nawang. Having been told of the traditional trading relationship between these Kenyahs and the Punan Oho, I asked whether the Punan received goods from the villagers in exchange for meat. My question was greeted with muted laughter; one old man replied, "No, the Punan never bring us meat. We Kenyah can hunt animals just as well as the Punan. We don't need meat from the Punan." I then asked what it is exactly the Punan do trade, and was told, *Barang hutan, macam-macam,* that is, "different things from the forest."

For the Punan Oho, and indeed for all of the Punan groups that I had occasion to study, these things have entailed a variety of natural products found within the groups' respective home ranges of primary forest. These natural forest products, or *hasil hutan,* commonly have included such items as rattan, resin, and fragrant aloes wood, along with rhinoceros horns and bezoar stones. Bezoar stones are concretions found in the internal organs or external wounds of certain animals. Punan groups have traded two types of bezoar, namely gallstones from certain species of monkey, and concretions that occasionally form around the external wounds of porcupines. Some groups—specifically the Punan Batu and Punan Binai, the Punan Murung, and the Punan of the upper Malinau River—also have traded edible types of birds' nests that are found in limestone caves within their respective territories. In addition, the Punan Murung have traded a wild nut that grows from several related species of tree found in their home range. Both the Punan Murung and the Punan Oho have traded minute particles of gold panned from the shallow headwaters of rivers in their respective areas.

With the exception of the Punan Batu and Punan Binai, each of the various Punan groups has traded its particular inventory of forest products with the sedentary agricultural people with whom it is affiliated and with whom it shares a common drainage area. The Punan Oho thus traditionally have been involved in trade with the Kenyah Lepo Tau. The Punan Lisum have traded with the Kenyah Lepo Timai, the Punan Berun and Punan Benyawung with the Kayan Malaran, and the Punan Kelai with the Segai. Punan of the Tubu have traded their forest products with the Tebilun; Punan of the Malinau have traded with the Merap. Each group trades its rattan, resin, aloes wood, bezoars in exchange for salt, tobacco, cloth, and metal implements.

Each of these Punan groups has provisioned itself with essential commodities and materials through a regular, ongoing trading relationship with a specific sedentary agricultural, village-dwelling people. Some of these groups have also, on occasion, bartered forest products with "other," more distant sedentary peoples, but neither has such trade been as friendly nor have the terms been as favorable as when the Punan groups have engaged in their normal exchange with their regular trading partners.

There are a few Punan groups who have traded some of their manufactured handicrafts with their sedentary neighbors, in addition to trading forest products. This is particularly true of the Punan Oho, the Punan Lisum, and the Punan Beketan, who on occasion received material provisions like *parang* and knife blades in exchange for their baskets, mats, and blowpipes. In fact, the Punan Oho have held to this day a sort of specialized monopoly in the making of blowpipes in their district, as the nearby Kenyahs do not make them and claim they never have. This is not true of Kalimantan in general. Elsewhere I found that sedentary Dayaks have made blowpipes as well as the local Punan.

This notwithstanding, forest products have been the major, and usually the only, items of trade among all the Punan groups I visited. It is easy to appreciate a Punan group's need for the goods and commodities it receives from sedentary people in exchange for forest products. An obvious question, however, is what do the sedentary people do with these forest products after they have obtained them from the Punan? The answer, though not quite as obvious as the question, is fairly simple: the sedentary people trade the forest products to someone else.

It is true, of course, that they do use a small portion of some of these forest products. Sedentary peoples have always had use for some of the rattan brought to them by Punan groups. Rattan cane is sliced into strips that are used for a seemingly limitless variety of household purposes; indeed, there are even some massively built, ironwood longhouses in the Apo Kayan area—some containing over thirty family apartments—that are held together with nothing but rattan lashing. Sedentary peoples also have used some of the resin. Prior to the introduction of kerosene lanterns and the now ubiquitous oil lamp, bits of hardened resin were used by peoples throughout Kalimantan to make rather smokey and dim, but long-lasting torches.

The sedentary peoples, however, have themselves had no use for monkeys' gallstones, concretions from porcupine wounds, or aloes wood. They have had no particular requirement for rhinoceros horns, nor have they much cared to sample the taste of birds' nests. They have known, however, that these items from the forest and the others we have mentioned are desired by "outsiders" or *Orang Luar*. They have known that such non-Dayak peoples as Malays, Buginese, and Chinese—outsiders from downriver—will gladly take these forest products and give things in return, namely metal, salt, cloth, clothing, tobacco, brass gongs, and large ceramic jars.

As such, unlike the trading relationships that prevail between, say, central African forest Pygmies and sedentary Bantu villagers (cf. Turnbull,

1965), the economic relationship between a Punan group and a sedentary agricultural village has not been directly symbiotic. The latter have derived little if any immediate benefit from most of the forest products brought to them by Punan, as they have had no direct use for most of these products. The sedentary villagers have instead reaped their returns in the goods and commodities given to them by outsiders in exchange for the forest products. And some of those goods and commodities, as we have seen, ultimately find their way back to the Punan group when the sedentary people trade for more forest products. We might say, then, that the trading partnership carried on between a Punan group and a sedentary agricultural group has been not directly symbiotic, but *ultimately* symbiotic.

The still nomadic Punan Batu and Punan Binai present an exception to this general pattern of economic activity, in that they do not trade with sedentary Dayak peoples. In their area, there are in fact none to trade with. These dispersed hunters and gatherers reside in coastal forest that is situated roughly midway between two large coastal market towns, namely Tanjung Selor and Tanjung Redeb. The Punan Batu and Punan Binai exchange their forest products directly with Muslim traders from the coastal towns. Those coming from Tanjung Selor make their way up the winding Sajau River; those from Tanjung Redeb travel up the Birang River and continue northward on foot through the woods. The Punan Batu and Punan Binai are thus host to an unending array of Balungan, Berau, Buginese, and occasionally local Arab traders desiring to traffic with the Punan on the Punan's own "turf." These Punan also differ somewhat from the other Punan groups of my acquaintance in their degree of specialization toward one type of forest product. For these coastal Punan, ranging through an area dotted with an unknown number of limestone caves,* the primary item of exchange is edible birds' nests.

We shall have occasion to return to this matter of economic exchange in chapter 3. We shall look more closely at these forest products and note their sources, uses, and ultimate destination. For now, let us conclude by noting that the collection and trade of forest products continue to play a major role in the lives of all of the Punan groups with which this study deals. For indeed, when settled Punan leave their villages to spend days or weeks in their former primary-forest territories, the collection of forest productions remains a principal motive for doing so.

Political Organization

There is an old assumption in anthropology known as the law of "limited possibilities." A frequently cited example of this idea is that there are only so

*Government records and traders' estimates place the number of caves in this area at roughly 100.

many ways to make a drum. Different peoples may use different materials, may employ different techniques, and may observe different conventions in style and decoration. But the desire to make an instrument that will be functional as a drum effectively limits and constrains the latitude for diversity and the amount of variation.

This example comes to mind as one considers the traditional pattern of political organization among the various groups known as Punan. For while the various peoples surveyed in this study have been widely scattered throughout eastern and central Borneo and have differed in language and ethnic affiliation, they have nonetheless been uniform in their present or former adaptations toward nomadic hunting and gathering. It is, as such, not surprising that a common form of ecological and economic adaptation should have generated fairly uniform patterns of social structure and political organization. As there are only so many ways to respond to the functional necessities of making a drum, there are likewise only so many ways to respond politically to a pattern of dispersed residence in primary forest.

The pattern of political organization we are about to describe reflects the former conditions of all the former and recent groups of hunters and gatherers that I studied; it reflects the present state of the still nomadic Punan Batu and Punan Binai.

Within a nomadic Punan group, each local encampment of two or three households usually featured one senior male as the head of the settlement. This was not a formal office. Whereas these forest encampments were normally temporary and ad hoc, the headship of an encampment was similarly a temporary and ad hoc position afforded to the man who, at that moment, best displayed such attainments as wisdom, goodness of heart (*baik hati*), the ability to influence others by word and example, and—perhaps most important—the ability to maintain peace and cooperation within the encampment. A man assumed the leadership of a settlement through personal attributes alone; he could neither inherit the position nor pass it on.

The head of a local encampment relied solely upon his personality as he attempted to exert influence. He had no real power. Instead, he was in effect primus inter pares—first among equals. He functioned as headman only during instances of decision making, during which his role was to moderate the discussion, interpose advice, and suggest possible courses of action. Generally speaking, final decisions were arrived at through consensus; during discussion, anyone who wished—man, woman, or child—could speak and air his or her opinion. The headman had neither the power nor the authority to impose his will upon anyone outside of his own immediate household. Moreover, once a consensus decision had been reached, no one actually was obliged to abide by it. A family always had the alternative of departing the present encampment to join another one or build its own. Also, among all groups aside from the coastal Punan Batu and Punan Binai, a family had the option of spending some amount of time in a village inhabited by affiliated sedentary people.

Beyond the level of the local encampment, political organization became more diffuse. This condition arose out of the fact that a nomadic Punan group was an amorphous unit with fluid composition and vague social boundaries. One might indeed be tempted to wonder whether a bunch of widely dispersed households, in only sporadic contact with one another and spread haphazardly over miles of dense jungle, was really a unitary group at all.

The fact remains, however, that the dispersed nomadic households conceived of themselves as belonging to a larger social entity on the basis of three unifying factors, namely *common kinship, common dialect,* and the identification with a *common geographical territory* at the headwaters and tributaries of a river. These three factors—kinship, language, and territory—operating simultaneously in the minds of people separated by miles of forest and difficult terrain, produced a loosely worn ethnicity or "consciousness of kind." It was this consciousness of kind, this sense of ethnic commonality, that formed a definite social unit of identity that we may designate as group.

Yet while the far-flung network of kinship through blood and marriage a common dialect, and the identification with a specific geographic territory generated a sense of group, these factors did not produce much in the way of political organization beyond the local encampment. A nomadic Punan group rarely acted in concert; indeed it rarely assembled together in one place at one time. Effective, structured group leadership did not exist. There was no real chief, there were no councils, nor were there general meetings to which all of the local encampments sent delegates. A Punan group was essentially an acephalous unit of identity.

There was, however, one definite, overarching, regulating mechanism that embraced the entire group: the ultimate interdependence of the group's component parts. It was this consideration, and perhaps this consideration alone, that effectively ordered the behavior of one individual toward another, thus ultimately providing a rudimentary sort of government that enveloped the entire group.

The rough demands and exigencies of tropical forest nomadism precluded any possibility that a lone nuclear family could expect to remain self-sufficient for very long. A nomadic family relied on other nomadic families for food, implements, news, and information concerning the location of game and forest products, as well as assistance in childbirth and remedies for illness and injuries. The young and unmarried needed to meet their counterparts of the opposite sex. In former times, furthermore, a family's dependence upon others was increased exponentially by the ever-present threat of intergroup warfare and headhunting.

Thus, at the same time that a diffuse pattern of residence and lack of overall leadership afforded wide latitude for dissension and nonconformity, the ultimate interdependence of the widely scattered members of a group provided a loose but definite constraint against excessively antisocial behavior. It was for this reason that the settlement of intramural disputes, involving such matters as adultery, theft, and violence within the group, often took the form of a public reaffirmation of the group's oneness, cohesion, and solidarity. Perhaps nowhere was this expressed more dramatically than among the several Punan groups of the upper Tubu area, where serious internal disputes were brought to a final resolution with a vivid symbolic enactment of group members' shared bonds of kinship. Within any one of these groups, a dispute settlement was made official by bringing the erstwhile belligerents together and inducing them to cut themselves and bleed into a common bowl. The bowl was then passed around and the blood drunk by all present to remind the disputants of their shared common blood.

Common kinship, common dialect, and common territory operated together to create a consciousness of kind and to define a group to its members. For each of the Punan groups described in this study, aside from the coastal Punan Batu and Punan Binai, there was yet another level of social inclusiveness beyond the group itself. As stated previously, each Punan group traditionally has been affiliated with a sedentary, village-dwelling, agricultural people with whom it has shared a common drainage area and with whom it has traded on an ongoing, regular basis. The Punan group has interacted with its neighboring sedentary people not only economically but culturally as well. Members of the Punan group have come to live in the village for varying periods of time and, for such groups as the Punan Kelai, Punan Oho, Punan Lisum, and Punan Beketan, intermarriage has often occurred between members of the Punan group and its affiliated sedentary people. The sedentary people have not only played host to "their" Punan and intermarried with them on occasion, but have also called upon the Punan to join them in war.

Punan Lisum and Punan Beketan frequently joined the Kenyah Lepo Timai when that group embarked upon war. The ancestors of the present-day Punan Berun and Punan Benyawung were regular and devoted allies of the Kayan Malaran. Punan of the Tubu were often enlisted by the Tebilun for the latter's raids against distant Kenyahs, and they moreover served in the role of sentinels of the Tubu River. From their vantage points in the forested hills above the riverbank, these Punan would scout advancing war parties entering the Tubu River and warn the Tebilun of impending attack.

In addition to coexistence in a common drainage area, the intermingling of peoples, economic interdependence, and alliance in war, a strong sense of ethnic similarity united a Punan group and a specific sedentary agricultural people. I was told by Kenyah Lepo Tau, for example, that they and the Punan Oho are descendents of one common ancestor. A similar tradition has existed between the Segai and the Punan Kelai, who maintain that their languages are almost identical and that they were once the same people. Among the Punan Lisum I was told, "Punan Lisum and Kenyah Lepo Timai have always had the same customs and almost the same language. We speak their language and they speak ours. We and they are the same people." While the Punan Kelai claim never to have fought against the Segai, and the Punan Lisum say they never have raised a weapon against the Kenyah Lepo Timai, these two Punan groups had no qualms about waging war against one another. The Punan Kelai and the Punan Lisum were traditional enemies and frequent opponents in war.

As such, the dispersed nomadic families of a Punan group conceived of themselves as belonging not only to their group but also, ultimately, to a wider circle of social inclusiveness that encompassed their affiliated sedentary people as well. This broader social unit, conceived of simply as "people of our kind," was cognitively distinguished from the surrounding cultural milieu made up of various "peoples of other kinds"—"other" sedentary peoples, and "other" Punan groups as well.

For the widely scattered households of a Punan group, this "people of our kind" category, comprising both the nomads themselves and the sedentary people with whom they were affiliated, entailed the maximal unit of social organization. It encompassed a tight, crosscutting web of personal interaction, economic interdependence, behavioral similarity, and cooperation in war. But just as there was no formal structured type of political organization beyond the local encampment that enveloped the Punan group itself, there likewise was no form of overarching political organization that exercised authority over this larger maximal social group as a whole. While there were indeed cases, especially in the Apo Kayan area, of some sedentary village chieftain referring to the local Punan group as "his" Punan, effective mechanisms of authority and control were all but absent. Instead, the adhesive element that bonded nomadic hunting and gathering families to a specific sedentary people was *ethnicity*. It was the deeply felt notion that, to paraphrase my Punan Lisum informants, "We and *these* village-dwelling people have always had the same customs and almost the same language. We speak their language and they speak ours. We and they are the same people."

Kinship and Marriage

As with all other native peoples of Borneo, kinship within Punan groups is reckoned bilaterally. The various groups of Punan that I studied have no descent groups of any type whatsoever, as the concept of descent itself is socially irrelevant. Punan generally are unconcerned with the notion of genealogy, and most are unable to remember their ancestors back beyond two generations. Structurally, a Punan group is essentially a loose network of overlapping, "ego-focused" personal kindreds.

Marriage customs are not quite as uniform among the various Punan groups as are the configurations of kinship. For example, marriage between first cousins is considered anathema and thus expressly forbidden among the Punan Berun, Punan Benyawung, Punan Kelai, Punan Oho, Punan Lisum, Punan Beketan, and Punan Murung, as well as among the Punan groups of the Malinau and Tubu rivers. Among the Punan Batu and Punan Binai, however, first cousin marriage is not only permitted, but highly preferred. Marriage between first cousins is referred to as "good marriage" by these Punan, among whom it is the preferential form. In this manner, I was told, the two families involved are never "strangers" to one another. Instead, marriage occurs between two households that *already* are close, cooperative, and on reasonably good terms. And moreover, the newlywed man and woman of such a marriage are far more likely to remain close to their parents than might be the case in other, less desirable forms of marriage.

Marked variation is also evident with respect to the custom of bridewealth. Among most of the native peoples of Borneo, marriage is normally contracted through payment of bridewealth. While there are occasional exceptions, such as the Merap people of the Malinau River—notorious in their area for not paying bridewealth when marrying either themselves or others—the overwhelming majority of the sedentary peoples of Borneo observe the custom of bridewealth.

Marriages are contracted through payments of bridewealth among some Punan groups but not others. The Punan Lisum, Punan Beketan, Punan Oho, Punan Murung, and Malinau and Tubu River Punan traditionally have paid bridewealth and continue to do so at the present day. Among the Punan Lisum and Punan Beketan in former times, the family of the prospective groom normally paid gongs and fancy, ornately decorated *parang* to the family of the prospective bride. Gongs and *sumpit* were the preferred items among the Punan Oho, and all three of these groups sometimes supplemented the normal items with ceramic jars of Chinese origin, known variously as *tempayan* or *tajau.* Among the Punan Murung, gongs and jars were considered *de rigeur* and occasionally were supplemented with small bits of gold. Marriage was especially expensive among the Punan groups of the Malinau and Tubu River area. While they were not unlike other Punan groups in the type of goods used for bridewealth, these Punan were exceptional by virtue of the sheer amount of gongs and jars they considered necessary as appropriate payments for marriage. Interestingly enough, these Malinau and Tubu River Punan have never thought it at all ironic that they pay relatively huge amounts of bridewealth while the nearby sedentary Merap people pay no bridewealth at all.

Money and modern appliances have largely supplanted gongs and jars as bridewealth goods among these various groups today. Among the Punan Lisum, for example, now settled in a government-run village near the town of Tabang, the custom has become established where, by 1980, a brideprice of as much as 300,000 rupiah (equal then to almost $500 U.S.) might be agreed upon. This price is met over a period of years through a combination of cash and goods. Such items as outboard motors, tape cassette players, shortwave radios, and wristwatches along with money have become the common goods of bridewealth payment among Tubu River Punan now settled in the vicinity of the large market town of Malinau.

At the other end of the spectrum are the Punan Batu, Punan Binai, Punan Berun, Punan Benyawung, and the Punan Kelai. Marriages within these groups, formerly and at present, have occurred without payment of bridewealth.

Among no Punan group of which I am aware is the custom of dowry observed.

Punan groups, nomadic and settled, exhibit no fixed rule of postmarital residence. Nomadic Punan will encamp wherever they have kin relations through blood or marriage; and the villages of settled Punan normally display an equal number of males and females who have married in from elsewhere.

Among all Punan groups it is the desire of newly wedded couples to obtain their own dwelling place immediately after marriage. Among nomadic Punan this desire is realized easily enough, as the newlyweds simply build their own *pondok* in whatever encampment they choose to call home. Among settled Punan, however, there is usually a brief period of waiting in which the couple reside in the house of either the bride's or groom's parents, or at the house of some other relation, until they are able to build a house of their own. Under ideal circumstances husband and wife are living in their own house around the time their first child is born.

Divorce—for whatever reason—is permitted and immediately obtainable among all Punan groups. Among some Punan groups, however, divorces are often followed by bitter arguments and recriminations over which of the two spouses was at fault, to determine how much of the bridewealth, if any, should be returned to the family of the husband. The Punan Murung of the Upper Barito area have worked out a useful solution to this potential cause of strife by ignoring the immediate question of blame. In general, if the wife initiates the divorce, all of the bridewealth returns to the husband's family. If it is the husband who decides to terminate the marriage, the bridewealth remains in its entirety with the family of the wife. As might be expected, divorce poses little problem among such groups as the Punan Batu,

Punan Binai, Punan Berun, Punan Benyawung, and the Punan Kelai, for whom there is no bridewealth at all.

Among the most common reasons for divorce among Punan generally are incompatibility, the waning of sexual interest, and the couple's inability to produce children. An especially common reason for divorce, however, is the serious offense of adultery. In former times, restitution in cases of adultery among most Punan groups was a relatively simple matter. The aggrieved husband—aided perhaps by one or two friends or kinsmen—pursued, captured, and murdered his wife's lover. It is nowadays the custom, however, for the man caught en flagrante to pay *dinda,* or penalty fines, to his lover's husband. These payments vary in amount and elaborateness from one Punan group to another. *Dinda* for adultery are likely to be nothing more than a couple of *parang* or *sumpit* among, say, the Punan Kelai; large payments of cash and gifts, and formerly gongs, are the rule among the Punan Lisum.

Dinda fines are similarly imposed in cases of premarital sex not leading to marriage. The family of the boy is expected to make adequate restitution to the family of the girl, adequate being defined according to the standards of the particular Punan group. In addition to requiring *dinda* payments, Punan groups of the upper Tubu River area, whose penchant for public drama was noted in the discussion of political organization, often smear the boy's body with the blood of a chicken or pig, "for all the world to see." The Punan Batu and Punan Binai tend to be more evenhanded. In a case of a sexual affair between two young people who subsequently fail to marry, effort is made to determine which of the two is blocking the marriage. If it is the boy who is refusing to marry, his family must pay restitution to that of the girl, If, however, it is the girl not wanting to marry, her family pays *dinda* to the family of the boy.

Childbirth and Child Rearing

Due to the rigors of their existence, the limited carrying capacity of their ecological niche, and a relatively high rate of infant mortality, the families of nomadic Punan are usually smaller than those of both settled Punan and other Dayak peoples. There are, on the average, about three children per family among nomadic Punan, while settled Punan families average around five.

Many Punan groups claim to have had effective traditional methods of birth control. Punan groups of the upper Malinau River area, for example, speak of having used a certain type of rare grass found deep within the forest. According to their accounts this grass was cooked and consumed in very small quantities with other vegetables, drunk with water or coffee, or simply eaten alone. It had, I was told, only to be consumed once, by both husband and wife, to prevent further pregnancies throughout the entire life of the couple. Interestingly enough, this grass is rarely sought or used at present, as these Punan now prefer to obtain conventional oral contraceptives at the local family planning office (*Keluarga Berencana*) in Malinau. "With the pill," as I was told, "you can always change your mind and have children," while the effects of the traditional grass remedy are utterly irreversible.

Abortion is not generally practiced, but infanticide has occurred among some Punan groups for babies born with serious and incapacitating birth defects. In addition, at least one group traditionally has made no effort to save the life of a baby born with its umbilical cord wrapped around its neck. Members of this group maintain that babies born in this unusual condition are sources of grave danger to their parents and to the group as a whole. There is reason to believe that this notion is not peculiar to this group alone—or indeed to Punan, as I was told by a Kenyah from the Pujungan district that his people have believed this as well.

Non-Dayaks residing in the coastal cities and large downriver towns of Kalimantan, many of whom never actually have seen a Punan with their own two eyes, enjoy relating many colorful and fanciful tales about the "Wild Punan of the Jungle." Among these tales is often the story of how a Punan woman gives birth. While the many anecdotes on this subject feature certain graphic variations, the general scenario that emerges is this. A bunch of naked Punan are on the march through the forest when suddenly, one of the women—naked and pregnant—begins to feel the first pangs of labor. The others continue their trek as she drops behind, gives birth to the baby alone, and then runs with her newborn child to rejoin the marching column, usually within the space of an hour after the birth. Variations upon this theme portray the woman as giving birth in a squatting position, cutting the umbilical cord with her machete, and then holding her newborn out to the dogs of the camp, who gather about and lick the baby clean.

The bare kernel of truth behind these stories is that there are and have been a few Punan groups in which women customarily bear children with little or no assistance and resume most of their normal activities after a few days' rest. Among most Punan groups, however, the act of childbirth differs little from childbirths occurring among sedentary peoples. The woman gives birth with the aid of at least one other woman, and at least a week passes before she is fully up and around.

It is generally the case among the native peoples of Borneo that a child is the object of almost constant attention and affection throughout the early years of its life. The Punan child is no exception. From the instant it awakens until the moment it falls asleep, the small toddler is held, caressed, cuddled, and petted. It is never spanked, rarely if ever spoken sharply to, or disciplined in any way, as it is not considered to be responsible for its actions. The life of the small child among Punan groups is characterized by the same indulgence afforded to children among every sedentary people of which I am aware.

This enviable state of affairs ends abruptly, however, at the birth of the family's next child, at which time the parents appear almost to lose interest in their older offspring, diverting their attention and affection to the newborn baby. At around the time it is five years old, the growing child is being assigned a steadily expanding share of small responsibilities, such as caring for its younger sibling(s), performing light chores, and running short errands. As the child grows older, it is gradually made to learn the full range of day-to-day activities appropriate to its sex.

While there are in actuality no rigid boundaries between the types of activity Punan consider to be men's work as opposed to women's work, girls tend to be induced to concentrate upon such domestic activities as cooking, mat weaving, food gathering, and infant care. Boys, meanwhile, are directing their attention to hunting, fishing, and such heavy work as the burning and clearing of swiddens. Thus by the time a Punan reaches middle or late adolescence, he or she has only to marry and produce a child in order to become a fully enfranchised, socially recognized adult.

Sickness and Therapy

Approaches to sickness and methods of therapy vary somewhat from one Punan group to another. Most Punan groups with which I am familiar know various traditional remedies for illness. These generally entail certain types of wood, roots, or leaves from wild plants, which are mixed with water in various ways and then drunk. Recourse to remedies of this sort is had for a variety of illnesses. In one village on the upper Barito River, for example, I encountered a young, newly married Punan who had seriously injured himself falling out of a tree. He had been perched in the tree's upper branches, picking fruit, when he lost his footing and tumbled to the ground far below. Unable to walk, defecate, or lie comfortably in one position for more than a few minutes, the young man was particularly concerned about inability to perform sexual intercourse with his new wife. His sole means of treatment, prior to my arrival, was an old soft-drink bottle filled with chips and slivers of wood, which he would periodically fill with cold water and drink. The young man credited this *obat kampung,* or village medicine, for having saved him from death in the days immediately following his accident.

Like the vast majority of sedentary peoples in Borneo, many Punan groups have, or have had, ritual healers who treat illnesses within the group through the medium of trance and spirit possession. And as with the sedentary peoples, Punan ritual healers are usually middle-aged or older, and of either sex.

The Punan Murung, for example, traditionally have been rife with ritual healers, each one famous for a characteristic display of trance behavior and a stock assemblage of occult paraphernalia. Punan Murung proudly relate many stories about their healers of the past, and it often seems that the magical power of any one of these individuals increases proportionately to the length of time that he or she has been dead. The Punan Murung explain this theme in their stories by saying simply that the healers of the present are just not as good as those of former times.

One long-dead healer of the Punan Murung is said to have been able to project his healing powers over great distances to cure the sick in far-off villages and encampments. Another was renowned for an "ancient magical shirt" that he wore while attending to the sick. It is said that when in a state of trance he would enter the river up to his neck and then emerge with the shirt completely dry. I myself witnessed a female healer—in an apparent state of trance—place her bare foot upon glowing embers of wood, which, I was told, is a common feature of her performance.

Individual healers are known also for their special accouterments. One may be famous for the use of gongs, while another is noted for a predilection toward the drums. One might commonly wear numerous bracelets on each arm which he or she clatters in snare-drum fashion while dancing, while another favors dancing with a single hornbill feather.

A healer treats the sick by calling upon *hantu,* or ghosts, who enter the healer's body during a state of trance. The healer assumes the identity and personality of the ghost that has entered his or her body. A healer is often associated with a stock repertory of ghosts that appear to that healer habitually. *Hantu* are invariably long-dead beings whom no one in the village, no matter how old, was ever acquainted with in life. Essentially, the *hantu* are vaguely drawn characters—caricatures really, bearing no actual connection to anyone alive. As one young Punan Murung man summed it up for me one day, "Our healers and our magic never fail to work for us as long as we believe in them."

A small handful of Punan groups have had neither ritual healers nor traditional medicines of any kind. The principal approach to therapy among these peoples involved the sick person simply sitting by the campfire to keep warm. This was previously the case among the Punan Lisum. It was only, I was told, when these people began to settle in permanent villages that certain individuals received the talent of ritual healing.

At the present day, when the Punan Berun are ailing, they generally make tracks for Long Telenjau, the nearby Kayan Malaran village, where they obtain medicines from the village headman. Punan groups living near towns also buy various nationally marketed patent medicines or, when seriously ill, head straight for the local dispensary. One man expressed his bemusement to me over the fact that his group's shamans blame the Punans' illnesses on ghosts and perform magic, while the doctors mention viruses and administer injections; yet either way, the man said, the Punan recover equally well.

Funerary Customs

Among most of the Punan peoples I studied, there is a standard, classic approach to death within the group. This characteristic funerary custom, or lack thereof, is another topic of mirthful anecdotes told about Punan by non-Dayak inhabitants of coastal cities and downriver market towns.

Within minutes after death, the person who has died is buried directly in the ground, after which everyone present immediately abandons the encampment. In some cases the deceased is simply left to lie in his *pondok* as his surviving friends and relations run quickly from the scene. They do this out of fear of the dead man's ghost. While this once widespread custom is rarely practiced now by Punan groups that have settled, it continues to prevail among the still nomadic Punan Batu and Punan Binai. Its occurrence has been noted by such earlier observers as Harrisson (1949) and Needham (1972) among Punan groups in Sarawak, and, interestingly enough, similar manifestations have been seen and noted among tropical forest-dwelling nomadic peoples elsewhere in the world (cf. Seligmann and Seligmann, 1911:122; Holmberg, 1950:87; and Turnbull, 1965:145).

My own observations and inquiries brought forth some notable exceptions to the general pattern. Punan groups of the upper Malinau and Tubu River areas, for example, are part of a larger areal culture complex that includes the settled Merap and Tebilun peoples, who customarily used to bury their dead twice. Among all of these tribes, the newly deceased individual was first interred in a wooden chest placed inside a rudimentary shelter built up in a tree. The body was then left to lie in state for one year, after which time the bones were retrieved, washed, placed within a large Chinese ceramic jar, and then reinterred in a finer "house" built atop a tree. Each of these two tree burials was accompanied by a ceremony—a small one for the primary burial, a larger and more elaborate one for the secondary burial.

Similarly, the Punan Murung, dispersed throughout the upper Barito area in Central Kalimantan, are likewise a component of a larger culture complex including the Siang and Ot Danum peoples.* These groups bury their dead only once, and always within a wooden chest placed in the ground. Custom dictates, however, that every death be elaborately commemorated with a major feast. This involves the sacrifice of animals, and it is sponsored by

*J.B. Ave (1972) is of the opinion that the Siang are in fact a subgroup of Ot Danum.

the nearest living relatives of the deceased. Ideally this feast is supposed to be conducted as soon as possible after the burial, but the inordinately high costs involved often prevent its occurrence before the passage of months or, in some cases, years after the actual death.

While the feast commemorates the death of an individual, the feast itself is commemorated by the construction of a wooden memorial. The size and form of this memorial is determined by the degree of elaborateness of the feast itself. Families sacrificing at least ten pigs for their funerary feasts are entitled to construct within the village a thin wooden memorial post, normally around twenty feet in height, with simple ornamentation on top. A family going all-out and sacrificing a water buffalo, however, is permitted the vanity of erecting a more ostentatious wooden statue, usually carved in anthropomorphic design.

The Punan groups of the Malinau and Tubu rivers and the Punan Murung of the upper Barito insist that they have been observing their respective burial customs since time immemorial. These groups have no recollection of ever having practiced the "bury-and-run" type of funeral in which interment of the deceased is followed immediately by the abandonment of the encampment.

Religious Beliefs

It is well known that the traditional *adat* religions of the sedentary Dayak peoples of Borneo are elaborate and complex.* They contain well-developed cosmologies, profuse mythologies, and imaginative theories of creation and ideas about the natural order. Each of these religions features a pantheon of deities, many of whom are conceived of anthropomorphically. There is often a supreme being, perhaps also a consort for the supreme being, and an assemblage of patron deities associated with a variety of day-to-day activities. More often than not, there are in addition many complicated rituals and public ceremonies, sometimes conducted by specialized practitioners.

The traditional religions of Punan groups are abridged, trimmed-down, or "portable" versions of those adhered to and practiced by their sedentary Dayak neighbors. The Punan have, in effect, extracted from these complex and elaborate religious systems the bare utilitarian essence needed to provide a supportive ideology for their relatively simplified way of life. They have, as it were, left behind such cumbersome and unwieldy elements as agricultural

*Several of these sedentary Dayak religions have been well documented and described in great detail. Those unfamiliar with these belief systems are referred first to LeBar (1972:147-97), to two excellent studies on the Kenyah by Whittier (1973) and Conley (1973), and to a monograph on the religion of the Ngaju people by Scharer (1963).

rituals, feasts that go on for nine days and nights, and cosmologies taking hours to recite properly, and have brought away with them instead one special aspect of sedentary Dayak religion that is perhaps uniquely suited to the rough exigencies of nomadic hunting and gathering, namely bird omenology.

Punan religious beliefs revolve mainly around omens gleaned from the flight patterns and calls of birds. Each and every Punan group possesses a small pantheon of certain birds that are believed to be able to communicate with human beings. They do this by flying overhead in a precise manner and by issuing various meaningful calls.

A Punan entering the deep forest to hunt game or seek jungle products watches and listens for advice. A certain bird flying overhead toward the left is a bad sign, informing him that the path he is taking is either devoid of game or fraught with danger. If the bird, however, flies overhead toward the right, this is a good sign that indicates that the presently trodden path is safe and will lead the man toward game and the jungle products he is seeking. The mental equation of left with bad sign and right with good sign is a deeply embedded notion shared not only by all Punan groups but also by every sedentary Dayak people with whom I came into contact.

Most of the spirit birds within the pantheon of any Punan group issue two or more variant calls. A bird has what is described as a good call and a *kasar* or coarse, bad call. Good calls are interpreted as auspicious indications of imminent success; bad calls are warnings of impending danger or failure. The plethora of calls heard in the forest from the various spirit birds bear a variety of messages for those who know how to interpret them. A call from one bird tells a man to halt for a day or two and make camp at his present location. Another advises that pigs will be plentiful if the man veers off toward the left. The call of another bird may warn him of danger at the spot where he is resting, while another forecasts a chance encounter with a seldom-met friend. Certain calls signify a crisis back at camp, directing the hunter to return home at once. Among the Punan Murung there is a certain bird which, when it is heard singing in the middle of the night, informs its hearer that a close relation has just died.

An elderly Punan Beketan from the upper Tuboq River in the Tabang district related to me the manner in which one of his ancestors became a legendary hunter of wild rhinoceros. The man, as I was told, was guided in his quest for rhinoceros horns by a succession of spirit birds, each bird guiding him safely to the care of the next. Their calls led him through the forest by many twists and turns, enabling him eventually to bring down a grand total of twenty wild rhinoceros—all of them tracked and taken with the birds' unflagging assistance.

As the Punan explain it, the calls and flight-signs of their spirit birds are simply a matter of friends helping friends. Punan regard these birds with fondness and respect. Most groups will not hunt or harm their special birds under any circumstances. The birds are seen as invariably helpful and concerned for the well-being of their human friends. Punan Beketan say that the birds that speak to them are more than mere messengers; some are capable of issuing calls that render their hearers immune to danger and invincible against enemies.

While many Punan have at present become nominal Christians or Muslims, depending upon the region in which they are located, most still retain varying degrees of belief in the spirit birds. They see no inherent logical conflict in this, and indeed perhaps there is none. As an old Punan Lisum explained it to me one day, "Since God cannot speak directly to human beings, he appoints the birds as his assistants to communicate with people."

In many districts and from many different groups I was to hear over and over again, "All Dayak people believe in these birds. It is not only Punan that believe in them." This is indeed true. Compare the religion of any one Punan band with that of its sedentary Dayak neighbors and you will find that the birds of the Punans' pantheon are also to be found in the religion of the sedentary group, but as somewhat minor characters. Thus, for example, while the Punan Oho of the Apo Kayan display reverence toward birds they call *Shishit, Ki'ing,* and *Telajan,* these birds similarly exist in the religion of the nearby Kenyah Lepo Tau, with somewhat diminished significance.

Many Punan groups, in addition to their belief in spirit birds, also profess a belief that the sound of a tree falling the forest, called *kayu reba,* and the cry of a small deer known as *kijang* are invariably portents of doom and impending disaster to whoever hears them. Again. casual inquiry among sedentary Dayaks reveals that these too are embedded deeply within their notions of the natural order.

But more importantly, there is the aforementioned mental equation of left with bad omen and right with good omen. This deeply entrenched notion is shared not only by all Punan groups of my acquaintance but also by every sedentary Dayak people with whom I came into contact.

As such, we are able to see that what constitutes Punan religion derives from sedentary Dayak belief systems. Rather than being essentially different from Dayak religion generally, the religion of Punan groups is a scaled-down version, stripped to a bare utilitarian minimum to serve the somewhat specialized needs of nomadic hunters and gatherers.

Indeed, if any one conclusion can be drawn from the foregoing ethnographic overview, it is that the above statement might as well be applied to Punan culture in general. Those readers familiar with Borneo and with specific Dayak societies may already have gathered that, rather than being in any way different or out of the ordinary, "Punan culture" is precisely what one would expect of *nomadic Dayaks.*

Figure 1. Borneo: Administrative Units and Boundaries

Figure 2. Major Cities and Towns in the Area of Study

Figure 3. Major Rivers in the Area of Study

Figure 4. Nomadic and Formerly Nomadic Groups Visited by the Author

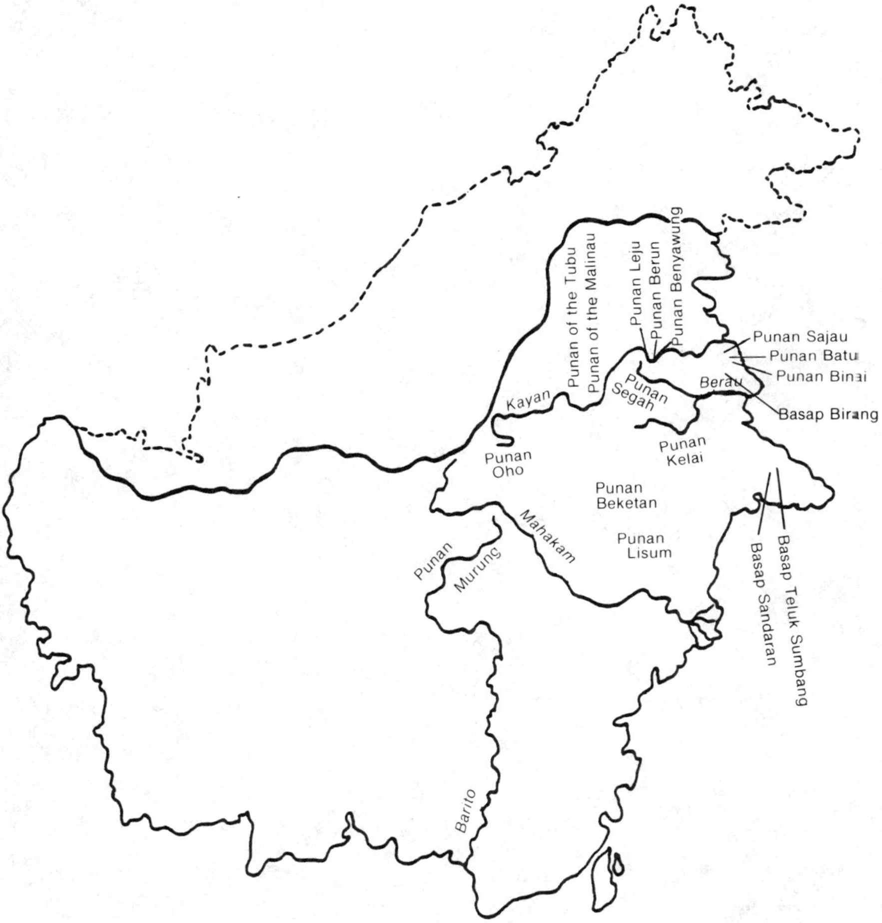

3

Punan: An Analysis

> I was intending to penetrate into the forest, and endeavour if possible to solve for myself the mystery of the Orang Poonan, or Wild People of the Woods. (Bock, 1882:69)

Fully one hundred years have come and gone since Carl Bock's brief encounter with Punan in the forests near Muara Wahau. Yet despite the passage of so many years, the "mystery" of the "Wild People of the Woods" has remained unsolved. If any common theme can be drawn from the various writings about Punan that have appeared at irregular intervals since the publication of Bock's narrative, it is that the Punan remained as much an enigma in 1982 as they were in 1882.

Anthropologists and others conducting research in Sarawak and Kalimantan have had difficulty making sense of the Punan for one fundamental reason. They have insisted upon seeing these people as being somehow distinct, outside, and apart from the general pattern of Borneo's traditional life. In the all too common conception, Borneo emerges as an island inhabited by Dayaks in the interior, Malays and Chinese on the coasts and—as a fast disappearing remnant of a long-vanished prehistoric era—the "Wild People of the Woods." As one author describes the Punan of Sarawak

> Their numbers are now very small; there are now less than 4000 in the territory of Sarawak; but they probably represent a race that at one time roamed over the whole interior of Borneo . . . they are adept at hunting, moving silently and invisibly through the jungle, and amazingly skilled in the use of the blowpipe. But they are timid and unaggressive. Down the centuries fiercer neighbours have encroached upon their ranging grounds, till now they are restricted to the forests round the upper waters of the Baram and Limbang rivers. (Runciman 1960:6)

This, in essence, has continued to be the standard concept of the Punan throughout the last one hundred years. That is, the Punan are the "aboriginals" of the island; they are "strange, unknown wanderers of the inner forests," and so on. Yet closer and more detailed examination of the problem reveals that the Punan are strange and unknown far more to anthropologists and travelers then they are to the various other Dayak groups of Borneo. Tom Harrison touched upon this point over thirty years ago:

> In general, Europeans and others still cling to the aboriginal or negrito theory.... The other peoples in the interior today do not normally regard the Punans as different in basic origin from themselves, only as much inferior. (Harrison, 1949:133–34)

Be that as it may, a close and prolonged inspection of the ethnographic picture in Borneo brings a significant observation to light. Not only do many of these sedentary agricultural Dayak peoples see nothing particularly strange or unknown about specific Punan groups living near them, they in fact regard these Punan as important adjuncts to their own way of life.

It is time to set aside our preconceptions about primitives, aborigines, and Wild People of the Woods, and to begin examining the Punan from the perspective suggested by the Chinese proverb that says "stare a long time at something strange, and its strangeness will disappear."

Neighbors and Friends: Sedentary Dayaks and "Their" Punan

> There is no way of getting in touch with the Punans or the other nomad tribes on their own grounds, but when wanted they always seem to appear. (Miller, 1942:69)

Upon considering the wide distribution of groups known as "Punan," one is stuck by the remarkable fact that these supposedly elusive, seldom seen groups can invariably be found living in relatively close proximity to other Dayak peoples. Punan groups, as can be plainly seen, do *not* wander haphazardly through the empty forests that span the length and breadth of Borneo. Rather, each group tends to confine itself to a fairly circumscribed area around the headwaters and tributaries of a drainage area that is inhabited in its lower reaches by a specific sedentary agricultural people. In the traditional pattern, we find the Punan group hunting and gathering in the forests upriver, and the sedentary group tending crops and building fixed villages downriver. Moreover, the dispersed encampments of the Punan group are generally no more than a day's walk from one or more of these sedentary villages.

The Punan Oho of the Apo Kayan area are able to reach any one of several Kenyah villages within the space of a few hours. Punan groups of the upper Tubu River were likewise only hours away from any Tebilun or Merap village they chose to visit. Punan Lisum in former times were never more than one day distant from the Kenyah Lepo Timai, and the Punan Murung of the upper Barito River claim to have never been more than a few hours away from the Siang and Ot Danum. As such, it has usually been the case that whenever a sedentary Dayak people wished to encounter members of their neighboring Punan group, they had only to paddle upriver.

The relative proximity of any one Punan group to one or more sedentary Dayak villages is reflected in the literature, even in that written by authors expounding upon the mysteriousness and elusiveness of the Punan. For even as Carl Bock insisted, "I believe these savages to be the true aborigines of Borneo. They live in utter wildness in the central forests of Borneo, almost entirely isolated from all communication with the rest of the world" (Bock, 1882:75–76), he was forced nonetheless to make note of the many "Poonans" he had found living for varying lengths of time at the nearby village of Long Wai, a settlement of the Modang people. These Punan "assisted" Bock during his stay at Long Wai by hunting game for him, rowing for him, and guiding him about in the nearby forests. When prevailed upon by him to do so, these Punan were able to bring Bock from Long Wai to one of their nomadic encampments in the jungle within the space of a few hours. Yet the obvious accessibility of these punan, and their nearness to the easily reached village of Long Wai, evidently did nothing to alter Bock's conviction that the Punan "live in utter wildness... almost entirely isolated from all communication with the rest of the world. Interestingly enough, however, the relative nonremoteness of the Punan that Bock met apparently did not go entirely unnoticed:

> I had often heard of the Orang Poonan, and of their alleged ferocity, and the state of utter savagedom in which they lived; and, though I had hoped to be able to see them in the course of my journey, I little expected to have been confronted with them so early. (Bock, 1882: 61–62)

We thus see that rather than hiding out in large expanses of empty forests, Punan generally lived in the same vicinities that other people inhabit—merely farther upriver, in tracts of primary forest. Whenever one finds Punan, it is virtually certain that sedentary Dayak villages will be met with not terribly far away. Conversely, vast stretches of forest that are devoid of Dayaks generally are correspondingly empty of Punan as well.

In addition to this proximity of Punan groups to their sedentary Dayak neighbors, there is the attendant factor of familiarity. Each group traditionally has stayed within a more or less circumscribed area, the group's home range, located upriver from a sedentary people to whom the Punan group is *well known*. The local Punan are neither a mystery nor an enigma as far as their sedentary neighbors are concerned. The Punan and the villagers maintain close personal relationships; individuals know one another quite well and address each other by name.

Furthermore, over and above the physical proximity and close bonds of friendship, the Punan group is also closely similar to its sedentary neighbors in customs, traditions, and usually language. Thus in the Apo Kayan area I was told by Kenyah Lepo Tau of one of their legends relating how they and the nearby Punan Oho are both descended from one common ancestor. The Kenyah Lepo Tau find nothing puzzling about this legend as they and the Punan Oho speak similar dialects and are culturally almost identical. These two peoples have been economically symbiotic for as long as anyone can remember. The Kenyah Lepo Tau informed me that they have, on occasion, traded also with members of such groups as the Punan Aput, but that the conditions are never as friendly or, as they expressed it, as normal as when they trade with the Punan Oho.

Another story of common ancestry was related to me by the Punan Kelai, who claim to be descended from the same ancestor as gave birth to the sedentary Segai. I was told by one Punan Kelai man, *Segainya hampir sama bangsa dengan kita*, that is, the Segai are almost the same people as us.

In the Malinau district I was informed by both Tebiluns and Meraps that their neighboring Punan are "the same as us—same people," a judgement with which every Punan group I visited in that area concurred. Tebiluns especially were eager that I should understand that the distinction between Tebilun and Punan was largely irrelevant to them. As far as they were concerned, they and their neighboring Punan were "People of the Tubu," some of whom lived downriver while others lived upriver.

In a village of the Ot Danum people, on the upper Barito River, I was told by one old man to stop worrying about who was Ot Danum, who was Siang and who was Punan Murung. He explained that while language varies slightly from one small village to the next along the upper Barito, all of the area's inhabitants nonetheless make up a single, uniform "type of people," with similar customs and historical traditions.

It is important to keep in mind the fact that non of these sedentary agricultural Dayak peoples feels any sort of kinship with Punan *in general*. The feeling of close affiliation that, say, the Tebilun have for the Punan of the Tubu does not extend to other groups in Borneo who are also known as Punan. A sedentary group's sense of affiliation is directed only to specific, neighboring Punan to whom those sedentary people are culturally similar.

A noteworthy example of this feeling of affiliation between a sedentary people and their Punan may be seen in the Peso district at the middle Kayan River, where the Kayan Malaran people refer to the Punan Berun and Punan Benyawung as "our little brothers." The Kayan Malaran, some forty years ago, abandoned their old swiddens, gardens, and villages and migrated to their present location from farther up the Kayan River. The Kayan now say that inasmuch as *they* were moving to a new place downriver, it was only natural that their Punan "brothers"—who were known in those days as the Punan Bahau—should pick up and move right along with them. As such, when these Kayan moved downriver and built their present villages at Long Telenjau and Long Naha Ayah, their Punan were staking out new primary forest territories nearby, thus becoming the present-day Punan Berun and Punan Benyawung. The former group interacts with the villagers at Long Telenjau; the latter with those at Long Naha Ayah.

The surprising correlary to this similarity and affiliation of specific Punan to specific sedentary peoples is the fact that any one Punan group is almost always closer in customs and language to its affiliated sedentary people than it is to other Punan groups living in other regions. Comparing the various Punan groups throughout the island, and one is immediately struck by the deep and profound differences relating to virtually everything other than their common habit of nomadism. And even in this nomadism, one will notice a genuine diversity in such baseline activities as hunting, fishing, and patterns of settlement and movement.

More striking is the broad divergence among Punan groups with respect to customs surrounding marriage, divorce, death, burial, and the treatment of the sick. It is a divergence of which the Punan themselves are aware. The Punan Oho of the Apo Kayan once insisted that I describe for them the customs and way of life of the distant Punan Batu. I obliged, and they shook their heads in astonishment as I did so. Punan Murung of the Upper Barito greeted my stories about other Punan with scornful laughter and exclamations of derision, one young man even going so far as to say that groups like the Punan Batu should be killed as they are an embarrassment to the country! In Malinau, a densely populated district (for Kalimantan) were Punan groups are correspondingly more numerous and consider themselves sophisticated, the Punan expressed an almost arrogant disinterest in the Punan groups I had seen in other areas, feeling no overt sense of kinship with them whatsoever.

But what Punan themselves find especially significant are the profound linguistic differences evident among the various groups known as Punan. While the Punan Murung, for example, have no difficulty speaking and understanding the languages of the neighboring Siang and Ot Danum, they are completely at a loss in trying to communicate with Punan they occasionally meet from the upper Mahakam River. One Punan Murung man informed me that the speech of Punan from the Mahakam sounds to him like the singing of birds." And, as mentioned previously in the discussion of language, two of my Punan guides in the Tubu River area, whose language is closely similar to those of the Merap and Tebilun peoples, related to me an anecdote about a previous chance encounter between them and some Punan from Central Kalimantan (most likely the Punan Murung). They told me that they and the "other" Punan were completely unable to communicate either in their respective native languages or in any native language the two parties knew, and that they finally were forced to converse in Malay. When I asked my guides why this should have been so, inasmuch as they were all Punan, they replied, "They were different people, not the same as us. Only their name—'Punan'—was the same."

Certain historical factors are interesting as well. Like Dayaks generally, most of the Punan groups of my acquaintance engaged in frequent warfare in former times. Many of these wars took the form of territorial disputes against other, different Punan. Perhaps the most warlike Punan group that I am aware of were the Punan Lisum of the upper Belayan River. By their own accounts, the Punan Lisum were willing to fight practically anyone and everyone, for any reason. As they expressed it, *Asal ketemu, langsung membunuh* ("If we met them, we killed them"). The Punan Lisum went up against other Punan with no less vigor and determination than that expended in wars against people of other tribes. When I asked them if there were not at least one people, somewhere, with whom the Punan Lisum were usually at peace, I was told that they never made war against the Kenyah Lepo Timai. I asked why this was so and was told, "Punan Lisum and Kenyah Lepo Timai have always had the same customs and almost the same language. We speak their language and they speak ours. We and they are the same people. But as for other types of Kenyah, like the Kenyah Lepo Tau, and other Punan, we fought them all the time."

Although they now rarely encounter most of the groups they used to fight, the Punan Lisum remember their old enemies in some detail. As I was informed, "We could always identify other Punan on sight. For example, the Punan Kelai all look alike. They are all very white and very, very big. They have muscular legs. They have broad bodies and are the best at using blowpipes. They can blow their darts farther than any other people." When I interposed the fact that many foreigners have always said that all Punan look alike, I was told, "not to us they don't. Other Punan look different, and each group has its own appearance—just as each group has its own language. Each group stands alone."

Finally, it ought to be pointed out that in addition to the common historical pattern of Punan waging war against other Punan, there are places in Kalimantan where an even more surprising situation has prevailed. Some Punan groups, albeit few, cannot recall having had much of any contact with other Punan at all. The Punan Batu for example, located near the coast of East Kalimantan, have only a hazy awareness of the very existence of Punan in other parts of Borneo, with the exception of a related band living somewhat to the south of them. This lack of knowledge is answered in kind by most of the other Punan groups, even those in an immediately adjacent district, who are equally unaware of the existence of the Punan Batu.

The question that thus emerges—a question perhaps more important to our understanding of the ethnographic picture of Borneo than many of us ever suspected—is *just who are these Punan and what are they doing here?* It is, if nothing else, evident from the foregoing that the term Punan means something quite different to Borneo people than it has meant to four generations of western travelers and anthropologists. For certainly the term seems to encompass a widely diverse and unconnected array of peoples who differ in language and customs and appear also to derive from diverse ethnic origins. What the groups so named do have in common is a present or recent habit of nomadism, along with the label Punan.

Something Amiss in the General Conception of the Punan

Before proceeding further, we should take due note of the fact that this surprising situation did not go undetected by everyone. As mentioned in chapter 1, several individuals at different times and in different localities throughout Borneo have observed that the Punan were not what they appeared to be at first glance. Let us pause for just a moment to consider some of these observations.

The use of the term Punan to designage a widely disparate assortment of groups was suspected well over thirty years ago by Tom Harrisson:

> [W]e do not even know if the person so termed really represent a culturally, a linguistically or physically related people, or whether they have several origins and are uniform only in a common habit of nomadism. (1949:131)

Exactly ten years after making this observation, Harrisson went on to clarify his position, adding what I believe to have been a remarkably astute bit of conjecture:

> [A]re the nomadic Punans or Pennans (or whatever it is) really so peculiar, so separate, just because they are nomadic and have (at present) a very special way of life? It is my own view that the Punans or Pennans (or whatever they are) do not differ fundamentally from the Kenyahs, Kayans and Kelabits, and that any one of these so-called "people," or all of them, could easily, under altered circumstances of nature, push out into the jungle and become nomadic as Punans. And, conversely that the people we talk of as Punans today do not stem from one simple and separate stock, but are themselves a reflection of not one but some of the now resident peoples around and among them. (Harrisson, 1959:133)

In addition to Tom Harrisson and his broad perspective on the Punan identity problem, there have been other authors who, speaking from their respective experience in small, widely scattered locales throughout Borneo, have noted the affinities of certain Punan groups to certain sedentary peoples. Odoardo Beccari, an Italian naturalist "wandering" through Sarawak in the years 1865 through 1868, expressed his puzzlement at an ethnic situation that greeted him at the mouth of the Belaga River:

> The inhabitants are called "Orang Skapan," and consider themselves as a distinct tribe, but I cannot see in what way they differ from the Kadjamans and the Kayans. All these tribal names in the Kayan country are, I think, nothing more than family distinctions, in short, what might be termed "clans." I could not otherwise explain how a few hundred yards from this locality, houses of Kadjamans, Skapans, Punans, and Kayans are found mixed up together. I believe that the Punans just mentioned must be considered distinct from those of the Bintulu, being much more civilized. (Beccari, 1904:302)

Punan of the Bintulu, Beccari had already suggested (ibid:285), were evidently akin to the "Mellanaos."

Charles Brooke, the second white Rajah of Sarawak, classified the Punan as a subgroup of the "Malanau" in the first volume of his lengthy memoirs. It is not clear on what basis he decided this, however, as in the second volume he went on to call them a branch of the Kayan people. (Brooke, 1866:I:73, II:301)

But we are on much firmer ground in the writings of Mr. I.A.N. Urquhart, former district officer of the Kapit area in Sarawak, who conducted a detailed genealogical analysis of the relationship between three nomadic Punan bands and the Kenyah Nyamok:

> [T]hese Kenyahs had lived at Long Dengan, where in a small river there are lots of mosquitos and hence the name Kenyah Nyamok. It was while these Kenyahs were at Long Pulen that Arang's daughter, while feeding pigs, had an unfortunate occurrence, for her cloths [sic] (presumably a traditional type of skirt) fell off revealing her completely and the people on the verandah, who witnessed the happening, laughed at her predicament. She and her husband Lawai were so ashamed at this that they ran off into the jungle and from them stem the present nomadic Pennan Silat, Pennan Talang, and Pennan Kelami (now settled Pennan Long Tebuku)....
>
> He also told me that the Nyamok and the Pennans are more or less the same and that in the time of his ancestors the Nyamoks lived half in the jungle and half in houses.... Tau Kampong Akam Laweng said "Libut was a Pennan or Nyamok, it is all the same, we are cousins." (Urquhart, 1957:113–14)

Government officials elsewhere on the island have made similar observations. From what was formerly Dutch Borneo, we have this remark from A. H. Spaen, who was Controlleur at Tanjung Redeb at the turn of this century, concerning Punan of the Berau area: "The Punans were considered by the Segais, in this case those of Muara Lassan, as sorts of members of the entire tribe... (Spaen, 1901).

J. S. Krom, Controlleur at this same outpost almost forty years later, made a study of the same groups. He found enough linguistic similarities between the Punan Kelai and the neighboring Segai to declare of the Punan: *"Zeer waarschijnlijk hebben we hier met slechts een stam te doen"* ("What we probably have here is a subtribe") (Krom, 1939).

Finally, a recently published handbook put out by the local government of the Kutai Regency in East Kalimantan classifies all of the Punan of that area as subgroups of Kenyah (Pemerinta Daerah Kabupaten Kutai, 1974:32).

We are thus able to discern that a small handful of individuals—mostly government officials of one sort of another—have noticed something amiss in the general conception of the Punan as mysterious, rapidly vanishing aborigines. Tom Harrisson was one individual who saw the problem in its broader perspective; Robert Blust of the University of Leiden is another. Blust has conducted fieldwork in Sarawak, a comparative linguistic study that led him to declare that "there are no linguistic grounds for regarding Penan dialects as distinct from Kenyah" (1972:13). More recently, he has employed linguistic inference to explicate some broader issues in Southeast Asian culture history. Blust argues (1976) that the cultivation of rice already was established as a mode of subsistence among Austronesian speakers prior to their migration and expansion. Thus, Blust suggests, the Punan of Borneo and such peoples as the Kubu of Sumatra, the Toala of Sulawesi, the Tasaday of the Philippines—indeed all Austronesian hunters and gatherers—were at one time sedentary agriculturalists who subsequently became nomadic.

The single, major roadblock that has hindered our ability to prove such assumptions has been the utter lack of comparative field data on Punan groups in general. Our understanding of the problem to date has been blurred by the fact that previously published information concerning Punan has been narrow in scope and highly specific to small individual localities. The resultant spottiness of our information regarding the Punan has left some important questions unanswered. If, as Blust maintains, the Punan of Borneo were originally sedentary and agricultural, then *why* did they subsequently desert their villages, abandon their gardens, and become nomadic hunters and gatherers—thus reversing the prevailing, "normal" direction of social evolution. And *what*, if anything, can so unexpected an occurrence tell us about the history of Borneo in particular and of human behavior in general? To quote Harrisson once again:

> What remains here is to determine how far, if at all, all the Borneo nomads . . . are originally interrelated. Are they of one stock, or do they reflect a series of separate responses to common environmental conditions and economic needs? This is one of the quite fundamental and fascinating unstudied problems of Borneo. Though difficult, and getting more so, modern transport offers a chance to tackle such a *comparative* study, which could illuminate the whole human process in equatorial Asia. There is a need for such studies. . . . (Harrison, 1975:4)

Such a study has now been made, and I believe that as a result of it we are presently able to answer some longstanding questions and resolve certain mysteries. I feel moreover that in directing our attention to the various whys and wherefores concerning the Punan, we shall be led to issues larger than the Punan themselves.

Specialization and Trade among Borneo Peoples

In September of 1980, quite early on in my fieldwork, I arrived at the village of Long Telenjau on the middle Kayan River. Although it is a village of the Kayan Malaran people, I had been told previously that I would be able to obtain there a boat and an escort to an encampment of the nearby Punan Berun. Like Carl Bock a century earlier, I was surprised at being "confronted" with Punan so soon. For there, in this Kayan village, were staying several Punan Berun, with others coming and going at frequent intervals.

In a little clearing adjacent to the house of the village headman, I noticed what seemed to be an enormous pile of raw rattan. This being more rattan than I had ever seen in one place, I asked my Kayan hosts what it was doing there. "We sell it to the Chinese trader in Long Bia," I was told, "and to other Chinese sometimes. Further conversation brought to my attention what in fact appeared to be a rather brisk trade in rattan between this village and a few chinese traders. Thinking that I had stumbled upon an example of "modern-day rural development at the grassroots level," I then enquired as to the age, sex, and number of the villagers whose job it was to gather the rattan for eventual sale, and was promptly told, "Oh, none of *us* gathers it. It's brought here to us by the Punan. They get it far, far in the jungle." I then asked whether all of the rattan sold by this village to the Chinese was brought by Punan and was told, "Yes, all from Punan." Thinking then that I had discovered in Long Telenjau some sort of entrepot, or collection center to which Punan from all over bring rattan, I asked my patient hosts which Punan groups they normally dealt with. "Only one group—the Punan Berun," they said, adding "The Punan Berun bring us this rattan, and they bring us *gharu* and *guliga* and other things, and we sell all of this to the Chinese." My mind racing, I did not bother at that point to ask them what *gharu* or *guliga* might be, as I now imagined that I was witnessing the modernization of a hunting and gathering band as a result of its absorption into an expanding cash economy. In that vein, then, I enquired as to how much money the Punan received in exchange for their rattan and "whatnot," and was told, "We give them salt, tobacco, and cloths—which they throw away—and all sorts of other things, but we don't give them money. What use have they for money?" Realizing now that I was quite out of my depths, I asked finally how many years this has been going on—thinking it to be some sort of recent arrangement—and was told, *"Sudah dari dulu, Tuan, Dari dulu dulu"* ("From long ago. Long, long ago").

The Chinese Presence in Borneo

> From the point of view of climate China consists of two distinct realms. In the north is the great plain, a land of hot summers and searingly cold winters, where a limited and uncertain rainfall combines with a short growing-season to restrict cultivation to one crop a year. Harsh though this environment is, it served as the cradle of Chinese civilization, the proving

> ground of the Chinese people. As soon as the Chinese polity extended its boundaries southwards, it gained control of a subtropical region of forested hills, with abundant rainfall and a year long growing season. Although the animal and vegetable products of this environment were profuse and various, there came a time when a developing desire for luxuries in a unified Chinese state could be satisfied only by the import of products alien to the soil of the country. At first these were brought in over the north western frontier, but even as early as the reign of Emperor Wu (141–87 B.C.) of the Former Han, Chinese imperial envoys with the help of men of Nan-yueh were exploring the South Seas in search of precious merchandise. (Wheatley, 1959:18–19)

> It is well known that trade long preceded the political and cultural conquest of South China by the Chinese. The Chinese exchanged their silks and other manufactured goods for luxury goods like ivory, pearls, tortoise shells, kingfisher and peacock feathers, rhinoceros horns and cinnamon and scented woods. With growing prosperity in the Huang Ho plains, the demand for these goods increased and this demand may have been the strongest single motive for the southward expansion of Chinese political power. By the end of the 4th century B.C., the Chinese had extended some control over the areas south of the Yangtse river. The final drive to the Nanhai, the Southern Sea, was only a matter of time. (Wang, 1958:4–5)

> The South China Seas have always been a Chinese lake . . . Wave after wave of people who had made their homes in China, including Indo-China, moved southward. There was never any political barrier in the prehistoric and early historic days. The only incentive was to make a living, especially when people were unable to do so in their homeland. The search for such an opportunity took them to all the havens and lands that they knew, and they did not hesitate to exploit any possibilities which they happened to encounter abroad. (Cheng, 1969:19)

> I would guess that wherever you go in the world, there will probably be Chinese. (An elderly Kayan from the village of long Naha Ayah, middle Kayan River)

It will most likely never be possible to determine with any certainty just when it was that the Chinese first appeared in Borneo. Historian Heine Geldern was of the opinion that Chinese contacts with insular Southeast Asia in general can be traced back at least to the first century B.C., and evidence from Borneo appears to have played an important part in forming his opinion:

> Taking all into account, one may come to the conclusion that direct Chinese influence in Indonesia goes back at least to the early Han period, that is at the very latest to the 1st century B.C. However, the ornamental designs of the Dyak tribes of Borneo and of the Ngada of Flores are so clearly related to Chinese designs of the late Chou period that one can hardly avoid the inference that Chinese contacts started as early as the beginning of the third century B.C., and probably earlier. (Heine Geldern, 1945:147)

In the absence of clear historical documentation, such options as these—however well informed—are of course only conjecture. To be sure, Chinese written records are virtually replete with references to the many faraway places visited by travelers, merchants, and imperial envoys; it is simply impossible, however, to say for certain exactly *which* places are actually being referred to. As O.W. Wolters has so wryly observed:

> If there is any activity which exposes one to the danger of being banished to the lunatic fringe of early Indonesian studies, it is the attempt to draw a detailed map of Indonesia on the basis of the information in the Chinese imperial histories. (Wolters, 1967:169)

Be that as it may, there has been no apparent lack of stalwarts willing to come forward and claim that certain of the place names mentioned in those imperial histories most likely refer to locations in Borneo. Concerning the land of "Chu-po," for example, a distant country mentioned in the accounts of K'ang T'ai and Wan Chen, two third-century geographers, Wolters himself insists, "This region [Chu-po] can only have been north eastern Borneo" (ibid: 52). Wolters also suggests that Borneo might be the identity of "P'u-lo-chung," described by K'ang T'ai as follows:

> One goes due east of *Chu-li*. If one goes to the end of the rugged headlands [one will find] that there are inhabitants on the sea shore. These people have tails five or six *ts'un* long. The place is called *P'u-lo-chung*. It is the custom of the people [there] to eat human beings. (Quoted by Wolters: 176)

What makes this passage so fascinating, to my mind at least, is the fact that stories concerning the existence of "a race of men with tails" persisted throughout the coastal areas of Borneo until well into the twentieth century. In fact, Carl Bock, assured repeatedly by coastal Malays that such people were actually to be seen somewhere in the interior," went so far as to form and lead an expedition—unsuccessful, as it turned out—to find them (Bock, 1882: 143–45 236–38).

It has likewise been argued that the "Yeh-p'o-t'i" mentioned in the fifth century by the celebrated traveler Fa Hsien, was actually a point on the west coast of Borneo (Braddell, 1949a), and that Borneo was also the location of "P'o-li," a fifth century kingdom that sent its first mission to China in the year 473 (Bretschneider, 1871; Braddell, 1949b). Sir Roland Braddell, basing his analysis on such navigational aspects as the direction of prevailing winds, was of the opinion that indeed many of the place and names mentioned in Chinese dynastic histories and travel narratives refer to locations in Borneo.

Moreover, Braddell has argued:

> [B]oth *a priori* reasoning and such data as we possess lead to a very early knowledge of Borneo on the part of the Indians and Chinese and that in the case of both of them probably, but the latter certainly, they must have been familiar with Borneo before they became familiar with Java, the navigation to which was far more difficult and more dangerous. (Braddell, 1941:72)

While such arguments are of course a matter of speculation, certain points are a matter of record and quite beyond doubt. Chinese coins of the Chin and Han dynasty have been discovered at the mouth of the Sarawak

River, and coins dating from the Sung period have been unearthed throughout the island (Runciman, 1960:13). Sepulchral pottery vessels from the Han period have also been unearthed (Purcell, 1951:15), and, as we shall note momentarily, hoards of Chinese pottery, some of it dating from the T'ang and Sung periods (Runciman 1960:13) have been kept as heirloom objects by Dayak peoples across the length and breadth of Borneo.

Archaeological excavations at Santubong in Sarawak attest to the existence of Chinese mining and smelting activity in that area during the T'ang and Sung periods (Cheng, 1969).

We know moreover that by the ninth century, the kingdom of Brunei—from which the island of Borneo derives its name—was already a prosperous trading entrepot known to the Chinese as Po ni. Chinese historical sources document not only the existence of this kingdom but also its gifts of tribute to the Chinese court in the year 977, and again in 1082.

By the twelfth century, Chinese sources are explicit and clear in their descriptions of regular Chinese trading activity in Borneo (Purcell 1951:28). This trade with China was similarly observed and described by some of the earliest European arrivals to the island. Antonio Pigafetta, who formerly had sailed with Magellan, visited Brunei in 1521 and made note of the Chinese silks and porcelains that he saw there, as well as the natives' adoption of Chinese weights and money (ibid.:448). Daniel Beeckman, trading at Banjarmasin in the year 1714, recorded his observations of Chinese ships and their cargoes (Beeckman, 1718:passim). Thomas Forest, a visitor to Brunei in 1776, noted his perceptions of that busy port as follows:

> At Borneo town the Chinese sometimes build junks which they load with the rough produce of the Island of Borneo, and send thence to China. I have seen a dock close to town in which a Chinese junk of 500 tons has been lately built. . . .
>
> Imagine a fleet of London wherries, loaded with fish, fowls, grain, etc., floating up with the tide from London Bridge towards Westminster: then down again, with many buyers floating up and down with them; this will give some idea of the Borneo market. (Purcell, 1951:487)

The long-term presence of Chinese in Borneo is further reflected in such place names as Kinabatangan—the "Chinese River," and Kinabalu—literally, the "Chinese Widow," the name of Borneo's highest peak. Also of some interest are the numerous stories and legends dispersed throughout the island concerning the alleged Chinese ancestry of certain Dayak tribes. Statements to the effect that the Murut and Dusun peoples of northern Borneo have been heavily infused with "Chinese blood" were recorded by such early travelers to the island's interior as Spenser St. John (1862, II:313), Sir Hugh Low (1893:172), and Odoardo Beccari (1904:253). Ascertaining the historical accuracy of these legends, and the precise degree of Chinese genetic contribution to Dayak peoples is, or course, quite beyond the scope of our discussion.* What is significant, however, is that these stories are very widespread and enduring. I myself heard several legends of this nature, some of them concerning Punan. Allegations that one or another Punan group are *campur dengan Cina*—"admixtured with Chinese"—are often part of the folklore about Punan that one hears from coastal Malays. Whatever their merit, these stories, along with the other evidence noted above, attest to a lengthy and continued Chinese presence in Borneo that has persisted down to the present day.

And having made due note of that presence, it now falls upon us to examine the anthropological result.

The Dayak Trade with the Chinese

> Tangible evidence of Chinese contact with Sarawak is afforded by the "sacred jars," undoubtedly of Chinese origin. The "jar cult" played an important role not only in Borneo but also among the Moi of southern Indochina, in the Philippines, in Formosa, and various other parts of the Indonesian region. (Purcell, 1951:27)

The importance of these sacred jars to the native peoples of Borneo has been documented and described in great detail by travelers to Borneo since the time of St. John (1867). It is well known that wherever one travels throughout the island of Borneo one cannot help but notice the many ceramic jars that are highly regarded and prominently displayed in Dayak villages by families of rank.

The jars that I saw most often in central and eastern Kalimantan were large stoneware urns, often well over three feet in height, invariably covered with a smooth chocolate brown glaze and further ornamented with a dragon design in relief slightly below the rim. I saw jars such as these in profusion particularly in the dwelling places of village headmen and in the homes of old men known as *Kepala Adat*—chief arbiters of custom, ritual, and traditional law. To even my unsharpened sensibilities it was immediately evident that these were heirloom items and greatly treasured symbols of rank, wealth, and prestige. I was told moreover that these *tempayan or tajau* as they are variably called have continued to be the preferred goods for bridewealth payments and indemnity fines, and that in some areas of Kalimantan they served as final resting places for the dead.

In addition to these dragon jars, appearing almost as a sort of adjunct, there were also brass gongs. Kept usually in the same corner of the room as the jars, heirloom gongs used in Indonesian gamelan orchestras were prized

* Those interested in acquainting themselves with the arguments pertaining to this matter are referred to Purcell (1951:25–26).

objects that were also favored for bridewealth and payments of indemnity. Almost as impressive as the gongs themselves were the ways in which they were conspicuously displayed. Headmen and others boasting sufficient numbers of gongs to do so liked to pile them up, one on top of the other, with the largest on the bottom leading to the smallest on top. Another mode of display that left one with no doubts as to who was the ranking member of the village was to be seen at a Kenyah longhouse, deep in the Apo Kayan. Here the widely renowned and venerable old *Kepala Adat* had taken one of his many gongs and placed it on the floor of the verandah, immediately outside his door. Visitors to the longhouse—not to mention its residents as well—were thus always greeted by the sight of a fine old gong serving as a doorstep to the great man's apartment.

None of the Dayak groups that I encountered can recall ever having made ceramic jars themselves; nor is there any recollection of having manufactured their own brass gongs. These items have come, either directly or ultimately, from Chinese. Also coming to the Dayaks from Chinese have been numerous items of necessity that most Dayak groups do not have and cannot produce for themselves.

One such item has been salt. This essential commodity is all but unobtainable throughout the interior save for a few localized, widely dispersed areas. The Lun Daya people of the Kerayan district, for example, have had their own natural sources of salt, as have the related Kelabit people in Sarawak. In the upper Barito vicinity there was similarly a saltwater spring about a day's walk from the most upriver villages, but its saline content was so low the people in that area only rarely had recourse to it. For these and most of the other Dayak peoples of Borneo's inland areas the chief, if not only source of salt has been trade.

Such has similarly been the case with metal. Among the Dayak peoples of my acquaintance, it was only the Kenyahs and Kayans of the Apo Kayan who could claim to have extracted and worked their own iron. Otherwise, it evidently has been trade, and only trade, that has kept other Dayaks of the interior supplied with metal for tools, weapons, and household implements.

Tobacco has been a particularly popular trade commodity for centuries. It was my observation throughout Kalimantan that Dayak men almost unanimously smoke, and many indeed are chainsmokers. Moreover, in the many areas of Kalimantan where adult men and women chew betel, rather large pinches of tobacco are taken in the same mouthful and chewed in conjunction with the betel, the lime, and the leaf. There are, to be sure, a few dispersed areas in which the local Dayak people somewhat indifferently plant and tend small patches of home-grown tobacco, certain villages in the Malinau district being one notable example. Here Tebiluns and Meraps have long grown, in somewhat haphazard fashion, their own tobacco, or *tembakau ong* as it is called. It is harsh, bitter, almost impossible to keep lit, and generally disfavored by the Tebiluns and Meraps themselves, who without exception prefer the tobacco they buy from shopkeepers and traders, thus relegating their own home grown variety to the status of tobacco of last resort. Elsewhere in Kalimantan the Dayaks are dependent on traders to assuage their hunger for tobacco, having not even the far less desirable alternative of locally grown leaves.

Similarly, Dayaks have long appreciated the appearance, comfort, and convenience of manufactured silk and cotton cloth, and they have generally held it in higher esteem than their own locally made bark cloth. More significant however, have been those occasions in which Dayak groups have had to turn to traders for food. This was often the case in historical times when tribal wars, forced migrations, and other disruptions prevented people from working their swiddens, thus obliging them to obtain rice from outsiders. While manmade catastrophes of this sort are today only memories, villages in some areas of Kalimantan must still purchase rice to supplement the occasional shortfalls of shifting cultivation.

We are thus able to see that the interior peoples of Borneo have for centuries been provisioned with materials obtained from Chinese. Some of these items have been largely of cultural and political significance, as in the case of jars, gongs, and such supplementary objects as finely polished beads of stone and glass. Accouterments of prestige, tangible symbols of rank and power, these objects have been reverently kept and conspicuously displayed, each item more often than not laden with its own legends and history. Yet other items—salt, metal, and sometimes even food—have been crucial to the continued functioning of Dayak societies and occasionally for the very maintenance of life itself.

These items and commodities obtained by Dayaks from Chinese have not been given as gifts or bestowed as tokens of fondness. Rather, these have been trade items received in exchange for other goods. Such goods have entailed a small inventory of natural, jungle products that Chinese have for centuries deemed valuable. It is this assortment of jungle products that has drawn the Chinese to Borneo for hundreds and perhaps thousands of years.

Now some of these products are not overly difficult for sedentary Dayaks to procure; indeed some of them, under ideal circumstances, can be located and gathered within a day's excursion from some villages. One such commodity is gutta percha, a rubbery latex obtained from the sap of certain trees of the genus *Palaquium*. Gutta percha has been a multipurpose substance that the Chinese have used sometimes for medicines, but more often as an adhesive and a waterproof caulking for sailing vessels. Aside from making things watertight, gutta percha has been put to such modern-day uses as insulation for electrical wires and cables. It also is used in dentistry.

Under ideal circumstances, the Dayak wishing to gather some gutta percha for eventual trade with Chinese has only to walk into the nearby woods and find the right tree. The man, or occasionally women, cuts the tree down, carves rings all along the trunk about two or three feet apart, and then collects the milky white sap as it oozes out from the rings. The sap is then brought back to the village and boiled, which hardens it into latex. The latex is then kneaded by hand, trodden under foot, and finally cut into chunks which are then tied together. Thus has the gutta percha been gathered, refined, and assembled for the trader.

Another forest product traditionally in demand by traders is the illipe nut. Roughly the same size and shape as an avocado, the illipe nut is known in Kalimantan as *buah tengkawang*. It grows wild in the forest and comes from several species of trees of the family *Dipterocarpaceae*. The Chinese, and some coastal Malays as well, have long valued *buah tengkawang* as the raw source of a rather greasy oil used for cooking. European arrivals to Borneo in the early nineteenth century, however, were quick to envision other uses for the oil. In his pioneering survey of Sarawak, Sir Hugh Low noted (1848:46–47) that oil from this nut was already being utilized in England to make tallow and wax; that it was proving itself serviceable as a lubricating oil for steam machinery "far surpassing even olive oil"; and that it also had been used by the Spanish in Manila in the manufacture of candles, where it was "found to answer admirably." Sir Hugh mused that this nut would most likely be found to serve other purposes in the future, and indeed it has. At the present day, it is gathered by Dayaks upriver, pounded and compressed by Chinese shopkeepers downriver, and then sent in the form of finished oil to the coast, where Chinese export firms sell it to European cosmetic companies who use it to make one of the world's most expensive varieties of lipstick. In 1968, the only year for which I have figures, the total income received by coastal export firms for the sale of *tengkawang* oil reached somewhere in the vicinity of $5,000,000 U.S. (Alexander, 1973:47).

Again, under ideal circumstances, sedentary Dayaks wishing to gather *buah tengkawang* have only to walk through the neighboring forests and pick the fallen nuts up off the ground. These are then brought back to the village, left out in the sun to dry, and eventually loaded onto boats and taken downriver to market. It is as simple as that—*assuming ideal circumstances prevail.* For if they do indeed prevail, sedentary Dayaks wishing to procure *buah tengkawang* or gutta percha will be able to gather these forest products in quantities sufficient for trade. Sedentary Dayaks are in need of the salt, tobacco, cloth, and metal that come from the traders; they have cultural and political need for the previously noted luxury items as well. The question is whether most sedentary Dayaks have been capable of gathering enough forest products, even such relatively accessible ones as gutta percha and *buah tengkawang*, to justify the time and energy diverted from the normal work of actual day to day subsistence. We might ask, in other words, whether most sedentary Dayak groups have been able to come up with enough forest products to bring in sufficient returns in trade commodities—enough forest products to make the energy expended in gathering them sufficiently worth the effort.

Generally speaking, the answer to these questions is, quite simply, *no*. The problem that arises, over and over gain, is that the ideal circumstances necessary for gathering forest products just do not prevail. For sedentary agricultural Dayaks, these ideal circumstances would involve proximity to forest products and sufficient time to go off in pursuit of them. These circumstances are, of course, closely interrelated in that the farther away the forest products are, the more time must accordingly be devoted toward searching for them and collecting them, time that would otherwise be spent in the day to day work for swidden agriculture. And as we examine the actual situation of sedentary Dayak life, we find that these two factors—distance and time—have in fact prevented most sedentary Dayak groups from being able to devote sufficient attention and energy to gathering the jungle products desired by Chinese traders.

The major fact that must be understood and kept in mind concerning virtually all of the jungle products desired by Chinese, and these will be inventoried in just a moment, *is that they are most commonly found within large tracts of primary forest*. Most sedentary Dayaks, on the other hand, are not.

In my own observations throughout Kalimantan, a sedentary Dayak village is surrounded by its gardens; the gardens are surrounded by swiddens; and the swiddens are surrounded by large expanses of *sedentary* forest, i.e., recent forest growing up over former swiddens. Primary forest, when any exists at all, is usually little more than a small remaining patch standing at the distant outer periphery of the village's lands.

This feature has been studied in close detail, and has even been quantified, in parts of Borneo that I did not visit. Michael Dove, studying the Kantu people of western Kalimantan, made some interesting observations concerning the nature of the ten square kilometers covered by the Kantu village of Tikul Batu (Dove, 1980). Approximately one quarter of this, he says, is given over to rubber trees, fruit trees, burial grounds, dwellings, and the combined surface area of trails and waterways. The remaining three quarters of the village's land is forest—ninety two percent of which is secondary forest (ibid.:15). Primary forest accounts for only the remaining eight percent, and much or perhaps all of this, Dove says (ibid.: 34), had in fact been cleared and farmed during the last century. Dove estimates, moreover, that each Kantu household clears an average of 2.3 new swiddens every year (ibid.: 6).

In many areas that I did visit, there are no patches of primary forest to be seen at all. What are seen instead are immense tracts of shadeless, tangled, secondary scrub forest that stretch for miles on end in all directions. In these areas, usually well populated, the large deforested tracts at the outer periphery of one village simply sprawl on to meet identical tracts at the periphery of another.

Thus, to make even the most haphazard attempts at gathering forest products, the sedentary Dayaks living in such localities must travel great distances to find primary forest areas in which these products are most likely to be met with. And given the nature of transport to such areas—on foot, or by boat through rivers often difficult to negotiate—a serious endeavor to gather forest products in quantities sufficient for trade involves an expenditure of days or weeks.

As it happens, this is time that most sedentary, agricultural Dayak groups do not have. The unavoidable requirements of swidden agriculture are quite time consuming. Each Dayak family must mark off its swiddens, clear away the underbrush, cut down whatever trees are standing in the way, set fire to the cleared underbrush and burn it away, plant crops in the swiddens, weed the swiddens, tend the crops, guard the crops against foraging wild pigs and other predators, and finally harvest the crops. During this process, and after the harvest as well, there are also the gardens to keep an eye on. A family cannot afford to sacrifice any of its manpower for repeated lengthy periods. Neither could a village afford to sacrifice much manpower in former times as any village stood constantly under threat of enemy attack.

Yet all the while, these sedentary Dayaks have been dependent upon trade commodities received in exchange not for the produce of their swiddens and gardens, but rather for an assortment of jungle products found far away in the primary forests. In addition to the gutta percha and *buah tengkawang* noted previously, these are:

Aloes wood. Called *Kayu gharu* throughout Borneo, aloes wood is the pathologically diseased portion of several different species of trees making up the genus *Aguilaria.* When burned, this wood gives off a pungent fragrance, and it has thus been used as incense by Chinese, Indians, and Arabs.

Edible birds nests. These finest edible nests are made entirely of a gelatinous, translucent, beige colored substance secreted through the saliva of a small swift (*Collocalia nidifica*). Another type of nest, regarded as quite inferior, consists of smaller quantities of this substance mixed with moss and other impurities, and is made by *Collocalia linchii*, a related species of swift. Called *sarang burung,* edible birds nests are small and found deep within caves, attached to the upper sections of the walls, close to the roof. Chinese use the nests in the preparation of various culinary dishes—soups, more often than not—and claim that the nests have medicinal uses as well.

Captain Daniel Beeckman, trading for the British East India Company at the port of Banjarmasin in the year 1714, introduced birds' nests to the English reading public as follows:

> Besides Pepper, they have Plenty of Birds nests, the best in the World, which are sold at 90 or 200 Dollars *per* Pecull; the whitest and clearest is the best. It is so call'd from certain Birds (much after the nature of a Petrell, or Swallow) which (as they tell us) having swallow's the Scum, Spawn, and Froth of the Sea, fly into the Holds of the Rocks, and high Cliffs near the Sea, where they vomit it, and beat it up with their Wings into a Consistency, which serves them that Season as Nests, (for they make new ones every Year) and after they have abandoned them, the Natives do gather them (being then a hard Substance) and sell them at the aforemention's price. This Birdsnest is counted a great Provocative to Venery. (Beeckman, 1718:146–147)

Bezoar stones. Generally referred to as *guliga* in central and eastern Kalimantan, bezoars are used for medicinal purposes. This practice has been a pan-Asian phenomenon, encompassing Chinese, Indians, Persians, and Arabs. Generally speaking, bezoar stones are the hardened concretions occasionally found in the internal organs of certain animals, especially ruminants. Borneo, however, has long been the source of two unusual and very valuable types of bezoar, the more common being *batu monyet*, or gallstones from monkeys. These are found, I was told, in the gallbladders of three varieties of monkey, and in perhaps no more than one out of a hundred of these monkeys that are hunted. Ranging usually from the size of a pea to the size of a lima bean, *batu monyet* has been known to occur in sizes reaching that of a small chicken's egg. They are inordinately valuable to traders; the larger the gallstone, the higher the value. Even more valuable, however, is the second type of bezoar found in Borneo, called *batu landak*. This type is a concretion that forms around external wounds in porcupines, and it is extremely rare. I was informed that only one out of "hundreds" of porcupines is to be found with such a concretion, and that porcupines themselves are encountered only occasionally, most often at night. *Batu landak* are always very small, extremely light in weight, and capable of fetching fantastic prices at all times.

These bezoars from Borneo, *batu monyet and batu landak*, have been valued for centuries by Chinese who esteem them as medicinals. Indeed, both varieties have been and continue to be the raw sources of an extensive array of pharmaceutical remedies for everything from stomachache to asthma. Beeckman, again, was probably the first European to publish information on the bezoars of Borneo. He mentions that they are of two types, from monkeys and from porcupines; he observes that the latter, "Golega Derre Landack," are of greater value than the former; and he notes that the natives "are very dextrous at making false Stones" in attempts to deceive traders (1718: 150–51). Carl Bock (1885: 206) states that bezoar stones in general "have been known in Europe for centuries," and he cites "I. Wittich, von den wunderbaren Bezoardischen Steinen, &c. Leipzig, 1592" as the oldest work in Europe published on the subject.

Rhinoceros horns. Like bezoar stones, the horns from the wild rhinoceros, called *tanduk badak*, have been thought for centuries to possess enormous curative properties. As such they have been pounded, pummeled, and ground up into a wide variety of Chinese medicines, including aphrodisiacs and treatments for impotence.

Resin. Known throughout Kalimantan by the Malay word *damar*, resin is collected from various dipterocarpaceous trees and used chiefly as an adhesive, as calking putty, and as a base for varnish. In former days, prior to introducing of the now ubiquitous oil lamp, hardened chunks of *damar* were used throughout the island for the making of torches. A small piece, supported by three sticks that were tied together at one end and set upright, gave off a rather faint, smokey light but could burn for over an hour.

Rattan. A modification of the Malay word *Rotan*, the term rattan covers several species of climbing plant that have been utilized in Borneo for everything from basket making to house building, and for furniture elsewhere in Asia and the rest of the world.

Camphor. Camphor is a modified form of the Malay word *Kapur*. Obtained in Borneo from the tree *Dryobalanops aromatica*, where it is found in hardened, crystalline form, camphor has long been used to make medicines and incense, and in embalming.

Beeswax. As its name implies, beeswax is a wax secreted by bees. Among the many uses to which it traditionally has been put by Chinese, beeswax has long been utilized in the making of base substances for a variety of ointments and medicines for external use.

Gold. In such locales as the middle reaches of the Barito, small particles of gold are panned from the river by Malays and Dayaks during *musim kamarau*, a short dry season that usually occurs in the month of August. Gold is panned all year, however, in the shallow headwaters of rivers and tributaries in areas such as the upper Barito and the Apo Kayan.

The fact that so many of these forest products have been used by the Chinese for specifically medicinal purposes should perhaps come as no surprise; this is quite in keeping with what we know about historical Chinese economic demands in Southeast Asia. In his signal study of Chinese trading activity in the South China Sea, historian Wang Gungwu (1958) has shown that the quest for medicinals, or raw materials for the Chinese pharmacopoeia, was a major impetus for Chinese contacts with the peoples of the "Nanhai." This was particularly the case, he says, during a three century period from the T'ang dynasty to the rise of the Sung.

We have seen the ecological dilemma faced for centuries by so many groups of sedentary agricultural Dayaks. Subsistence farmers in need of trade goods, unable to make a regular practice of leaving their villages, swiddens, and gardens for time consuming forays through distant expanses of primary forest, these sedentary peoples have all too often been incapable of gathering the forest products valued by traders on any kind of efficient, long-term basis. The sporadic, haphazard, "one shot" excursion to the deep forest by one or two sedentary Dayaks—no matter how successful—could hardly be expected to net their families sufficient returns in essential trade goods, much less provision their village.

Homo sapiens is a resourceful species, however. For this dilemma was greatly alleviated, and sometimes even resolved, with just the sort of sociological adjustment one would expect of human groups adapting to their environment. In many parts of Borneo, and at many times in history perhaps, the Dayaks appear to have done precisely what one would expect them to do: *they specialized.*

Having done that, they have continued to present the picture that greeted Carl Bock on his arrival at the Modang village of Long Wai over one hundred years ago—a picture that has similarly greeted the arrival to Borneo of four generations of anthropologists and others ever since: a sedentary Dayak village, tending its gardens and swiddens, and receiving forest products from a culturally related group of nomads from the forests upriver, whom the villagers call Punan.

The Punan–Sedentary Dayak–Chinese System of Trade

In its barest outlines, the system works as follows throughout central and eastern Kalimantan. A Punan group ranges its home territory hunting, gathering, and collecting forest products. The Punan, at irregular but frequent intervals, bring their forest products to one or two villages inhabited by a sedentary Dayak people with whom this particular band of Punan traditionally has been affiliated. The sedentary Dayaks receive quantities of one or more of the valuable jungle commodities listed above. In exchange for these, the Dayaks give their Punan "little brothers" quantities of salt, tobacco, and cloth or machetes, in amounts they consider appropriate, depending upon what and how much they have received from their Punan. A few pieces of *damar*, or resin, need be exchanged for nothing more than a few blocks of salt and a couple of bags of tobacco; a bezoar stone may well demand some machetes or perhaps even a gong, depending upon its size.

When the goods have been traded—and news and gossip have been shared, and conversation has been sufficiently exhausted—the Punan will gather up their small quantities of trade goods and return to the forest. The sedentary Dayaks, for their part, will paddle downriver and exchange the forest products for much larger quantities of salt, tobacco, metal, and such household implements as pots and woks. If the forest products are of appropriate amount and quality, the Dayaks may well be rewarded with a jar or a gong as well.

The trader bestowing these items upon the Dayaks in exchange for the jungle products is either a shopkeeper of Chinese descent, or a coastal Malay or Buginese entrepreneur plying the lower reaches of the area's larger rivers in a boat. Either way, the trader encountered by the sedentary Dayaks is merely a middleman in the forest products trade, running a small-scale operation from a town situated at the broad lower stretches of the area's major river. His livelihood, modest but comfortable, derives from assembling the forest products brought to him by the sedentary Dayak villagers upriver, and then bringing these raw commodities down to the nearest city on the coast, where he will sell them to one or more large export firms owned and operated by Chinese. While he is in the coastal city, the trader will use some of his profits received from the export firm to restock his supply of those items necessary to continue his trade with the sedentary Dayaks upriver; salt, tobacco, cloth and clothing, metal goods and such "trinkets" as large ceramic jars with glazed surfaces and dragon designs.

It is worthwhile noting that right down to the present day, the peoples at either end of this Kalimantan trade route—Punan and urban Chinese exporters—have had in most cases little or no awareness of one another's existence. Yet all the while, the jungle products have found their way from the forests to the coasts, and the trade goods have filtered through from the coasts to the deepest recesses of the forest, for centuries unnumbered.

Having gotten now a basic grasp of the trade system in its broadest, most general outlines, we will examine it for a moment more closely. It begins, let us say, in the eastern forests of the Peso district of the middle Kayan River area, where a small group of people are encamped near a narrow stream. They are a family belonging to a group known as the Punan Benyawung. For weeks they have been hunting, fishing, gathering wild fruit, and collecting rattan and aloes wood. The food they have gotten from hunting and gathering is for their own subsistence, but the *rotan and gharu* are for their "older brothers," the Kayan people of the village of Long Naha Ayah. These Punan have no idea why the Kayans of this village always seem to want these and other jungle things, but they know that the villagers will give salt and tobacco in exchange for them. The man of the family has long needed a shirt, as the one that he is wearing is dirty and torn. While he knows that no one in the village will give him a shirt for the rattan and the few small pieces of *gharu* that he has, he decides nonetheless to bring his things to Long Naha Ayah now, as he is in need of salt and completely out of tobacco. So he brings his wife and his four small children to a nearby encampment and leaves them behind there, proceeding onward to the Kayan village alone. Arriving at Long Naha Ayah, the man seeks out one or two Kayan men with whom he has always been close. They tell him, however, that they have nothing much to trade for the *rotan* and *gharu*, and they suggest that he go to the *Kepala Kampung*, the headman of the village, saying that if anyone in the village has enough salt and tobacco to trade, it will be he. So, after passing the idle hour in conversation with his two Kayan friends, during which they sat and passed a small plastic bag of tobacco and cigarette papers among them, the man walks on to the house of the headman, who, after a bit of perfunctory haggling, takes the rattan and the aloes wood and gives him eight blocks of salt and five plastic bags of tobacco replete with rolling papers. The man sleeps that night at the house of one of his friends and leaves the village on the following morning. At the encampment in the forest, later that day, his family and friends are quite pleased with the salt and tobacco he is dividing up amongst them. "It was a very good trade," they all say.

"It was a very good trade," says the Kayan headman to his family back at Long Naha Ayah. For if the Punan were pleased, he is virtually delighted. Although he knows that the demand for rattan has been rather low in the area lately, he can tell by looking at the *gharu* he has just received that it is of the rare quality designated as *nomor satu*, or "number one," by the old Chinese shopkeepers down at Long Peso. It is valuable *gharu* and will doubtlessly fetch a good price from the Chinese, while all of the rattan that the Punan have brought to him these last several weeks probably will not. He is not too concerned, however, because he knows he has something else the Chinese merchants will prize. Wrapped in a little piece of cloth kept safely in a suitcase under his bed is a small bezoar stone from a monkey. It was brought to him over a month ago by another Punan Benyawung, a third cousin of the man that has just brought him the *gharu*.

Tomorrow the headman will take the bezoar stone and the *gharu*, along with as much rattan as he can load into his boat, to the very old Chinese man whose stone is the biggest in Long Peso. With the money he receives in exchange for these goods the headman will buy much salt and bags upon bags of tobacco. He will also buy some shirts and some medicine, for he promised these to the Punan man who brought him the rattan and *gharu*. If there is any money left over, he will put it safely away in that suitcase under his bed. He is saving money to buy a large ceramic urn to give to the father of the girl his oldest son wants to marry.

When he has brought the jungle products to the big store in Long Peso and has sold them all to the Chinese, he will think no more about them. He does not know where they will go from Long Peso or what will become of them. Like the Punan people who bring these jungle things to him, the headman has no idea why the Chinese merchant—or anyone else for that matter—wishes to buy them, and he has never in fact given the matter much thought.

We shall stop this only slightly fanciful narrative here, before it goes unnecessarily far afield. The readers, if they are so disposed, can use their own imaginations, to envision the labors and vicissitudes of the old Chinese merchant as he assembles the forest products he has bought from sedentary Dayaks throughout the area and sends them to the coast by boat. It is enough that we have seen the forest products safely on their way from the Punan to the sedentary Dayaks, and then on to the middleman trader in town.

In this examination of a sample transaction, we have watched the basic processes or a trade network that apparently has continued in this manner for centuries. The only real change that modern times have wrought is the introduction of money as a common basis of exchange, supplanting the older system of barter.

Each of the scattered Punan groups brings forest products to its affiliated sedentary agricultural people. In exchange for these, the Punan group receives from the villagers smaller amounts of trade goods that the villagers themselves have obtained from the traders with whom they deal. The Punan as such, are a living example of the "trickle down theory," as they receive their noticeably reduced allotments of salt, tobacco, clothing, metal implements, and, less frequently, gongs and jars.

As we have seen, trade between sedentary Dayak villagers and their Punan generally is conducted on an individual basis and not between whole groups. It is most unlikely that one will encounter anywhere in Kalimantan the spectacle of an entire Punan group and a whole sedentary village meeting en masse at a clearing in the forest. Nor is a Punan group likely to file into a village as a body for trade. Rather, what happens is that a Punan Oho, for example, may visit a Kenyah friend at the latter's longhouse in the village of Mahak Baru. He may bring a quantity of *demar* and receive a few blocks of salt and some tobacco in exchange. Some weeks later when this kenyah leaves Mahak Baru for a brief visit to a market town downriver, he will bring the *demar*, along with whatever else he may have gotten from this or other Punan friends and acquaintances, and sell the whole parcel to a Chinese or Malay trader. Nowadays the *demar* and other products would most likely be sold for cash, in former times the Kenyah would have bartered it for whatever essential or status items he required.

In theory, Punan arriving at the village of a related settled tribe have had the right to trade their jungle products with any and all of the villagers, *siapa saja yang mau beli*, that is, whoever wants to buy. In actual practice, however, it has often been only the village headman and other high ranking individuals that have had the wherewithal to trade with the Punan for their valuable jungle products. It has often, in other words, been only the wealthy who could afford to become wealthier. It is the man already rich in gongs who is best able to part with one, to exchange it with a Punan for a rhinoceros horn that will earn him more gongs in exchange with traders. The jungle products gathered by Punan have often perpetuated and widened the class and wealth distinctions in sedentary Dayak tribes.

Until relatively recently, there have been few direct contacts between Punan groups and traders in most of the interior areas of Kalimantan, beyond some occasional chance encounters. They have traded indirectly, with sedentary Dayak groups standing in between. Not surprisingly, sedentary Dayaks have done little if anything to foster such encounters, preferring instead to keep their Punan and the traders away from each other. They have no doubt always been aware that any sort of direct trade between Punan and the outsiders would make their own mediating position redundant, if not unnecessary. While the traditional pattern is beginning to break down, as many such direct trading relationships already occur in Kalimantan, groups like the sedentary Meraps of the Malinau district adamantly refuse to tell their settled Punan neighbors how much money they have been getting from selling forest products to the Chinese.

Interestingly enough, however, I found that the sedentary peoples have scarcely greater knowledge than their Punan neighbors concerning just what it is the Chinese do with the forest products once they have gotten them. Up until the moment I myself told them, none of the various peoples I met had any idea, for example, that bezoar stones are wanted to make Chinese medicines, that aloes wood becomes incense, and that birds' nests are used to make soup. Nor was anyone aware that rattan is exported to foreign countries all over the world in the form of expensive furniture.

Variations in the Pattern

As noted in the previous chapter, some variations on this general pattern are to be seen in several hunting and gathering groups that live in coastal areas of East Kalimantan. There are a surprising number of these groups, and they are considered locally by virtually all who know them to be the most primitive peoples in that province today. These include the Punan Batu and Punan

Binai of the district of Tanjung Palas, a closely related group known as Basap living a few miles to the south in the Gunung Tabor district, and two more groups referred to by the same name living in the hills directly above the coast in the districts of Talisayan and Sangkulirang in the Mangkalihat peninsula. While these last two groups of Basap are linguistically identical and in fact genetically related, they apparently are distinct from the Basaps living far to the north of them in Gunung Tabor, or whose existence they are quite unaware. What all these groups have in common is an almost total nomadism that has persisted to the present day, along with a traditionally pervasive and direct economic relationship with coastal people and coastal people only.

A prime example of these coastal groups are the Punan Batu, or Stone Punans, so named for their habit of seeking temporary shelter in the caves where they gather birds' nests. Still nomadic, they range a home territory at the headwaters of the Sajau River, not more than a few miles inland from the Celebes Sea. Up until the Second World War, these coastal forest nomads gathered birds' nests for the Sultan of Berau. His agents would come from Tanjung Redeb, the Sultan's seat, to collect birds' nests from the nomads for eventual sale to coastal Chinese. The proceeds from this little industry appear to have made up a not inconsiderable portion of the sultanate's annual revenues. In exchange for gathering the birds' nests from deep within "his" caves, the Sultan, through his agents, kept "his" Punan Batu supplied with salt, tobacco, and little else.

The sultanate passed into history shortly after the Second World War, and the Punan Batu now gather their birds' nests for a variety of coastal traders—Malays, Buginese, and sometimes even Arabs—all of whom sell the birds' nests to coastal Chinese, exactly as before. And in exchange for gathering the birds' nests from deep within the caves, the traders keep the Punan Batu supplied with salt, tobacco, and little else. A portion of this group has settled into a government-supported village on the middle reaches of the Sajau River, where they live in houses, grow rice, and, for the most part, no longer consider themselves Punan.

Those who are still nomadic, however, are almost totally specialized to one role in life, the gathering of birds' nests for coastal traders, upon whom they are virtually dependent. Farther to the south, in the Gunung Tabor district, the closely related Basap of the upper Birang River are dependent upon coastal traders not only for salt and tobacco, but for the means of remaining nomadic as well. These people do not and cannot make blowguns; they have no one among them who knows how to manufacture them. The coastal traders supply the Basal Birang with blowguns so that they may subsist in the forest while gathering birds' nests. The traders obtain the blowpipes from farther in the interior, but the Basaps have no idea where.

There are other groups of this sort in the coastal forests of eastern

Kalimantan. Of different origins and linguistically distinct, they all nonetheless present two striking characteristics: a primitiveness unusual even for present day groups of Punan, and a constant and unremitting orientation to the requirements of coastal traders.

When we step backwards a few paces to view these coastal nomadic groups within a larger ethnographic perspective, one that encompasses all of eastern Borneo, we are presented with a grand picture that seems to stand in defiance of all our expectations. Most anthropologists would presume that peoples living in the interior would be somehow more primitive than those living near the ocean. In the minds of westerners generally, four hundred years of exploration and colonization have firmly established the notion that the deeper one journeys into the "dark interior" of an exotic land, the more culturally pristine the people there are likely to be. This entrenched assumption, moreover, is held by nonwesterners as well; many coastal Malays, Buginese, and Chinese who are unfamiliar with the interior districts of Kalimantan have always assumed, and still do assume, that mankind could display no people more wild and primitive than the Punan of the island's deep interior.

Reality has a way of intruding, however. Not only are these notions not true, the *exact reverse* is in fact the case. As one leaves the interior of eastern Kalimantan and travels down the major rivers to the coast, one finds that the Punan begin to appear more primitive, not less so. The closer one gets to the coast of East Kalimantan, the more materially impoverished and behaviorally simplified the Punan seem. What is more, this is an almost steady retrogression in appearance, accelerating and becoming more pronounced as one draws nearer and nearer to the eastern coast.

Strange as it may seem, the most modernized and assimilated Punan groups of East Kalimantan are those dwelling in the remote and relatively isolated Apo Kayan and upper Mahakam River areas. These areas have always been difficult to get to from points downriver. Only within the last ten years, for example, have the airplanes of the fundamentalist Protestant Mission Aviation Fellowship simplified travel to the Apo Kayan from the coast. Access to the region by boat up the Kayan River is hindered by a long treacherous stretch of boulders and white water rapids, impassable for all but the smallest boats that can be lifted up and carried around the maelstrom. The upper reaches of the Mahakam are similarly hard to navigate with most types of boat; in fact, news of a man's capsizing and drowning reached me during my own visit to the area. Yet, the Punan groups of these regions are settled in proper villages, live in well built wooden houses with corrugated aluminum roofs, and have abundant gardens and swiddens. They wear store-bought, factory-made clothing, and have wristwatches and combination cassette tape players and shortwave radios, on which they listen to Indonesian language broadcasts of the Voice of America. They are, by all standards and appearances, virtually indistinguishable from other Dayak peoples in their areas. Of one group, the Punan Oho of the Apo Kayan, I heard one young Kenyah Lepo Tau man say, "They're not really Punan anymore, are they?"

As one moves eastward, however, one encounters the more traditional, semi nomadic Punan groups of the upper Malinau and Tubu River areas, of the middle Kayan, and of the Segah and Kelai Rivers. All of these areas fall within a broad north-south arc about midway between the center of the island and the eastern coast. They all, moreover, share a relative proximity to market towns and traders. Even the most remote locality among these areas, the upper Tubu, is no more than a two-day boat trip downriver, at most, to the town of Malinau. This large river town boasts two hotels, numerous stores, a post office, electricity from 6:00 P.M. until midnight, schools, churches, mosques, several households owning large console television sets, and now, I am told, even a movie theater. And yet all of this notwithstanding, the many Punan groups residing in this area—and there are quite a lot here—are by and large only nominally settled. With the exception of one rather fancy government-built and government-supported village at the nearby Sembuak River, the villages of Punan groups in this area are rather more like base-camps from which whole families fan out for weeks at a time, hunting and collecting forest products to trade with the merchants and shopkeepers in Malinau. The settlements of Punan groups of the middle Kayan and of the Segah and Kelai Rivers farther south are generally characterized by an odd sort of dwelling—a small hut, some of it bamboo and some of it wood, that is slightly too permanent-looking to be a jungle *pondok* and yet not substantial enough to pass for a village house. And roughly half of these stand empty at any one time, their inhabitants being off in the forest for days or weeks on end.

This remarkable process of increasing traditionalism culminates as one arrives at the coastal areas and encounters the truly nomadic groups of the forests near the sea. These surprising people still live in tiny shelters made of sticks and leaves, and some, like the Punan Batu, take up their habitations in the mouths of caves. They continue to wear loincloths, often made from bark that they gather and pound into cloth. Their possessions are few and among their most cherished items are discarded bits of rubbish from the world that impinges only miles away. Among my most vivid recollections from visits to these groups are women and girls wearing steel safety pins as earrings, men carrying their tobacco in former talcum powder cans, a family storing bits of clothing in an old plastic bag that displayed the Xerox corporate logo in faded blue and white, and an old man treasuring an heirloom Chinese abacus.

One of these groups, roaming about the forested hills above Teluk Sumbang in the Talisayan district, lives literally on top of the coast. They are reachable by a forty-minute walk—all uphill from the beach at Teluk Sumbang. One can in fact see the ocean in the distance from some of their *pondok*.

The Punan Batu and Punan Binai, meanwhile, are so close to the coast that helicopters flying to and from the Atlantic Richfield Company's offshore oil installations pass over their encampments several times a day. These nomadic, cave dwelling, hunting and gathering Punan are potentially within a one-day motorboat trip—or a fifteen-minute helicopter ride—from Tarakan, a large coastal city containing sizable numbers of American and European expatriate employees of foreign oil companies and oil-related industries. These company employees, working in Tarakan and patronizing its hotels, restaurants, nightclubs and bars, have never heard of the Punan Batu and Punan Binai. They are quite unaware that they fly over such people several times a day during their helicopter shuttles to the oil rigs.

We have here, as such, a problematic situation that seems to contradict not only the popular western notion that primitivism is a function of geographical remoteness, but also some specifically anthropological ideas about the "erosion of traditional ways of life" in the face of outside influences. In what manner indeed are we to explain why Punan groups appear increasingly more primitive and culturally pristine the nearer one gets to the coast, and why conversely they seem more and more modern and assimilated the deeper one trudges into the island's interior? An answer—perhaps even *the* answer—emerges when we remember just what it was that made these people what they are; when we consider the social ramifications of the activity that turned the ancestors of these people into groups of Punan. That activity, of course, was *trade*.

Stated simply, the closer a Punan group is to the coast, the more accessible it is to coastal traders, the more oriented it is to the traders' requirements and demands, and the more dependent it remains upon the goods that they provide. On the other hand, Punan groups that are farther away, relatively remote, and less easily accessible to traders have had both the time and the incentive to diversify their economies and grow out of their traditional ways of life. For these groups farther into the interior it has simply been a matter of joining the present-day, mainstream movement toward change that is in evidence among all of the other Dayak peoples of the interior, a movement whose pull has been stronger than that exerted by older values.

For those groups whose niche has been the coastal forests, however, time and impetus for change have been in noticeably short supply. In those forested hills above Teluk Sumbank, Malay, Buginese, and Banjarese traders are constant and frequent callers, requesting rattan from the Basaps, for which they often pay in advance. The Punan Batu, who in former days gathered birds, for the sultans of Berau, nowadays do so at the frequent behest of coastal traders from Tarakan, Tanjung Selor, and Tanjung Redeb. These and the other groups of the coastal areas continue to maintain an appearance that strikes the observer as primitive in the extreme.

But the primitiveness of these people is merely in the eye of the beholder. It is essentially nothing more than an artifact of western ethnocentric preconceptions about distant lands and nonwestern peoples. This primitiveness, moreover, has nothing whatever to do with our usual notions of unilinear social evolution, in which human groups are seen to evolve from nomadic hunters and gatherers to sedentary agriculturalists. Appearances, as the saying goes, are often deceiving; and the primitiveness of these coastal forest hunters and gatherers is indeed a matter of appearance.

It is trade, I say again, that has been what these Punan of Borneo are all about. It is trade, I believe, that has generated the particular type of hunting and gathering adaptation known to three generations of western travelers and scholars. It is trade that has created and perpetuated a specific ecological niche that has been occupied by groups of people known as Punan. Thus, if these various coastal and near-coastal groups appear to us as somehow more primitive than those of the island's interior—looking, in effect, more Punan like than all of the other Punan, it is simply because the coastal groups are that much more specialized in the activity that turned sedentary Dayaks into nomadic Punan—the collection and trade of forest products.

Punan and Commerce

The fact that Malays and Chinese trade with sedentary Dayaks, and sedentary Dayaks trade with Punan has by no means been overlooked by anthropologists, travelers, and others. Numerous individuals have in fact witnessed and described isolated types of trade transactions occurring in certain places between specific groups.

The earliest reference to Punan of which I am aware, that by Spenser St. John, indicates quite clearly that one person at least noticed the economic role of these people as far back as 1862:

> In the neighbourhood of the Kanowit, and scattered about these countries, are the wandering tribes of Pakatan and Punan, which seldom build regular houses, but prefer running up temporary huts.... They are the great collectors of wax, edible birds' nests, camphor and rattans. (St. John, 1862, I:45)

St. John went on to note that these peoples "are the true manufacturers of the Sumpitan, or blow-pipe" (ibid.).

Even Carl Bock, as early as the 1870s, had noticed the prevalence of trading activity in eastern Borneo, and he noted it in his book, albeit in somewhat haphazard manner. When he arrived at the city of Samarinda, for example, at the beginning of his journeying through Borneo, Bock noticed

> The commerce of Samarinda is very considerable. Everyone is a trader, even the Pangerans and the Hadjis. Here, as everywhere, John Chinaman musters in great force, and the greater part of the export trade is in his hands. At the time of my arrival there were five vessels—three of them barques of considerable size—all belonging to Chinamen, being loaded with the produce of the country, which is brought down the river on long rafts. Rattan is the staple product; but gutta percha, timber, beeswax, and edible birds' nests (*Sarong boerung*)... are also exported in considerable quantities. (Bock, 1882:25–26)

A bit later on, when he reached the upriver town of Muara Pahau, he saw that the Malays living there

> do a large trade with the Dyaks, who come down with their produce—rattan, gutta, and edible birds' nests, and occasionally a couple of the precious bezoar stones—to exchange or sell, for the Dyaks are beginning to fancy the Dutch silver *ringits*.... (ibid.:127)

Bock was aware, moreover, from having been told by the sedentary Modang, that such forest products as birds' nests and bezoar stones normally were gathered by "the Orang Poonan, and that the Orang Poonan (the forest people) are the chief collectors of wax" (ibid: 205). He noticed that the Punan received machetes and cloth through trade with the villagers at Long Wai (ibid.: 74–75), and he perceived such sundry bits of ethnology as the Dayaks' intense fondness for Chinese glazed jars (ibid.: 197) and their ignorance concerning the ultimate use for bezoar stones, which they "sell at such fabulous prices to the Malay traders for the Chinese" (ibid.: 214). As it happened, however, Bock did not connect these many perceptive but disjointed observations.

Odoardo Beccari similarly managed to notice at a quite early date, his travels occurring between the years 1865 and 1868, that the Punan

> Make very fine mats; but this is, I believe, their only art, though they are great collectors of wax, camphor, gutta-percha, rotangs and edible nests. When they have exhausted the produce of a locality they move on to another. (Beccari, 1904:264)

He also made due note of the fact that Dayaks consider "precious" (ibid.: 265) such items as Chinese jars and gongs, and went on to argue:

> The hypothesis that the Chinese knew and traded with Borneo at a very remote epoch has gone on gaining ground, supported by new facts which all tend to prove its truth .... In 1888, at Santubong, at the entrance of the Sarawak river, fragments of gold jewelry, crockery ware, glass beads, stone crucibles and ancient Chinese coins, some of a period as far back as 600 B.C., were discovered.... The *tajau* jars, so precious now to the Dayaks,... and perhaps certain ceramics found amongst the Mellanaos, also come under the head of Chinese antiquities. (ibid.: 365)

In a somewhat different vein, we have the following observations on trade between sedentary Dayaks and Chinese written by what appear to have been early tourists to the island. While somewhat coarse and unflattering, the comments are noteworthy in that they suggest that trade between Dayaks and Chinese was important enough and pervasive enough to have been noticed by even the most casual observers. We thus have these notes from Sarawak:

> A Chinese trader came to the village to-day, to trade rice for gutta-percha, wax, etc. The Dyaks are either very stupid, very lazy and shiftless, or all three together. Instead of taking their gutta down to Kuching, where they could sell it at 60 cents per cattie (11/3 pound), and buy rice at ten to eleven gantongs for a dollar, they loaf around the village until a sharp Chinaman comes along and takes their gutta at 37 1/2 cents per pound, in exchange for rice at five gantongs to the dollar, and cheats them in the weight of both! (Hornaday, 1894:433)

This theme is echoed in the following profile of the Chinese trader in Brunei:

> He goes out singly or in pairs in his clumsy row-boat far up to rivers where savage chiefs reign undisturbed over tribes of naked brown men . . . and seemingly regardless of the fact that he might pay forfeit for his temerity with his head, proceeds to swindle every man jac, of the blood-thirsty tribesmen of their stores of gum, wax, rubber, rattans and other articles of value. He weighs the articles in his own scales, which all present are aware are doctored in his favour, and pays them all with tobacco, knives, cotton cloth, looking-glasses, and beads of hardly any value at all. (Blundell, 1923:126)

But the "long-suffering Dyak" appears to gain the upper hand in these observations from Kalimantan:

> When a Dyak has a bezoar to dispose of, he assumes a kingly attitude like unto that of an exclusive dealer in diamonds or pearls. He allows it to be noised about that he has one or more such "priceless jewels" in his possession and leaves it to his fellow Dyaks to convey this information to the first Chinese trader that visits the kampong. It is beneath his new dignity to approach the Chinaman. The Chinaman must come to him, as he sits in kingly state before his apartment of the tribal *lamin*. In the transaction that is sure to follow, the dyak does not, like the Chinese or other Orientals, haggle and dicker, but sets his one price, which he will not reduce in the slightest, regardless of all discussion and argument. The Chinaman simply must come to his terms. It is gratifying thus to see the Dyak, in selling bezoar stones, score one on the slant-eyed trader. But eventually the Chinaman gets even when, with a stock of tinseled ornaments and other baubles, he revisits the Dyak settlement just before a celebration of the Feast of the New Year: (Krohn, 1927:315–16)

During the succeeding decades, as travelers narratives gradually gave way to the in-depth analyses of government officials and anthropologists, the many disjointed bits of information did, in time, come to be connected and interrelated. Their significance with regard to Punan, however, remained obscure. I.A.N. Urquhart had a clear understanding of the economic relationship between "Pennans" and sedentary Dayaks, but failed to see this as being of any importance to our understanding of the forest nomads, even though he long suspected that "the Pennans are just another one of the tribes of Kenyahs" (1959:75).

With much greater detail, Rodney Needham discussed the nature of trade between "Penan" and "Kenyah and other overlords at their longhouses on the rivers" (1972:178), yet he too stated no opinions concerning any significance this may have beyond simple economic exchange.

In his brief survey of settled Punan and Bukat in the upper Kapuas area of West Kalimantan, Victor King noted:

> Jungle products such as the illipe nut and damar are important items of exchange, and during the illipe nut season Chinese traders are fairly frequent visitors to these remote villages. They also come for the gold which is obtained by Punan and Bukat from shallow streams and outcrops along river banks. (King 1974:41)

King provided no other information on economic exchange, but he did make due note of the following observation:

> The Bukat and Punan are linguistically and culturally distinct, as are the Penihing... formerly they had their own well-defined hunting and gathering grounds. However, within these categories there is also marked linguistic and cultural variation, between, for example, the Punan of the Keriau and those of the Bungan. (ibid.: 39)

In wider perspective, Tom Harrison (1949:145) described a complete sequence of trade in forest products, from Magoh Punans to sedentary Berawans to Chinese, apparently without perceiving the significance of this trade in relation to his basic, long-held belief that Punan stem originally from sedentary Dayaks. More recently, Jerome Rousseau offered this outline of the system in general:

> We may consider briefly the nature of the relations between agriculturalists and nomads. It is based on commerce... Traditionally, the settled groups have offered cloth, iron, tobacco and manufactured objects against jungle produce and handicrafts which are then sold to Chinese traders. (Rousseau, 1975:41)

There is, I believe, a rather serious deficiency in these and other observations concerning Punan and commerce. For in the usually described, commonly presented scenario, trade is mentioned almost parenthetically as just another thing that Punan do. One almost derives the impression from some authors that Punan would rather be doing almost anything else, especially chasing wild pigs through the length and breadth of the forest.

Punan are variously pictured as "afraid of the sunlight," "averse to emerging from the shade of the jungle," and "timid and shy in the presence of settled Dayaks." But all the depictions agree on one essential point: "They need to trade with the settled peoples, however, in order to remain nomads" (Needham, 1972:177–78).

The point suggested by my own observations is precisely the reverse. Punan do not trade in order to remain nomads; they have instead remained nomads in order to trade. Punan do not collect forest products to support themselves while hunting; they hung—and gather the fish—to support themselves while collecting forest products. Trade is not just another thing the Punan do; it is essentially *the* thing that Punan do. It is, I believe, the collection and trade of forest products, and not hunting, that historically has been the raison d'etre of nomadic, primary forest groups known as Punan. It has been both the demand for these forest products and the local need for the goods they bring in exchange that have led to the hunting and gathering adaptation that modern-day westerners have observed—the existence of groups called Punan.

The popularly held assumption that the Punans live deep within the jungle in order to hunt animals for food is refuted by the somewhat surprising observation that wild pigs and other game animals are often just as plentiful in downriver areas and near large towns as they are in the primary forest. In fact pigs are often more plentiful near villages than in the forest, on account of their attraction to the gardens and swiddens of the villagers. Dayaks living downriver in or near such towns as Malinau, Long Bia, Tabang, and Tumbank Kunyi often told me of having to guard their swiddens against foraging wild pigs and mentioned the difficulty of preventing the pigs from ravaging their fruit gardens at night. Although there are not many references to this point in the literature, the following remark, almost ninety years old, suggests that what is true now was likewise the case in the past:

> Wild hogs were so plentiful in the jungle that the Dyaks had built a pole fence four feet high around three sides of their clearing to protect their crop of rice. (Hornaday, 1894:395)

Moreover, one can often observe wild deer drinking at riverbanks not more than five kilometers from any of the towns mentioned above.

As such, Punan groups would have had scant cause to dwell in primary forest areas for hunting considerations alone. Rather, Punan groups have dwelt in the deep forest areas because it is there that most of the jungle products they collect and trade are to be found. As for their nomadism, let us simply recall the comments of Odoardo Beccari: "[T]hey are great collectors of wax, camphor, gutta percha, rotangs and edible nests. When they have exhausted the produce of a locality they move on to another" (Beccari 1904:264).

The Name Punan

Before closing our analysis of the Punan, it might be instructive to consider once more certain adjacent issues that were touched upon earlier in this study, such as the name Punan itself. Having examined in some detail the matter of *who* the Punan are and what they appear to have contributed to the traditional social milieu, some readers may still be asking themselves the following question: If the so called Punan of Borneo are in fact a diverse array of widely scattered, unconnected, unrelated, culturally and linguistically dissimilar groups who, in some cases, are often unaware of each other's very existence, then why are they all called Punan?

To begin with, let us realize once again that many of the so called ethnic names in use throughout the island are in fact what Borneo anthropologists call exonyms. An exonym, stated simply, is a name conferred upon a group of people by members of other groups, in contrast to whatever name—if any—the group calls itself.*

The exonym phenomenon occurs the world over and is hardly restricted to Borneo alone. But it is in Borneo that we so often have the added touch of a single exonym referring to several and sometimes many groups at once, groups often totally dissimilar and unrelated to one another. Consider, for example, these comments concerning the ethnic name Murut:

> The term Murut ("hill-people") is applied in Borneo to two completely dissimilar sets of ethnic groups, neither of which uses the term itself. In Sabah it refers to the groups inhabiting the Interior Residence south of Keningau (who are known in Sarawak as Tagal); while in Sarawak it refers to the groups living in the Lawas and Trusan areas of the 5th Division (known in Sabah as Lun Daye).... Linguistically, the two Murut sections have little in common. (Prentice, 1972:154)

and these, concerning the so called Tidong:

> It is doubtful whether all, or even most, of these people identify themselves as Tidong. They appear instead to comprise a heterogeneous collection of local populations, many of differing ethnic origins, who have adopted similar patterns of coastal or riverine settlement and a common set of religious institutions derived from Islam, and who have been identified by neighboring groups as constituting a separate category, distinct from both the non-Islamic interior people who surround them and the other Muslim groups living in close proximity along the coast. (Sather, 1972:167)

---

* While racial epithets and offensive ethnic terms come readily to mind as examples of this phenomenon, exonyms are not necessarily insulting. They may be mildly pejorative—as in the use of the term Quakers to refer to members of the Society of Friends, or they may be neutral—as in the use of the word Cheyenne to refer to a tribe of Plains Indians who called themselves *Tsistsistas*—"The People." What is usually the case, however, is that the exonymic term is quite different from that used by the group itself for its own name.

and this, with regard to the Melanau:

> The word "Melanau," like "Malay" and "Iban," is not a word traditionally used by the peoples we now know by that name, it was used by Brunei people, and others, to refer to the pre-Islamic, but later much Islamized, peoples of coastal Sarawak. . . . (Babcock, 1974:194)

and finally, this statement concerning the name Kenyah:

> The word "Kenyah" is simply a gloss whose content varies according to the area. The criteria of linguistic similarity and presumed common origin identify *some* groups who are universally classified as Kenyah, but the same criteria cannot define *all* those to whom the term "Kenyah" may apply. (Rousseau, 1975:37)

My own observations brought a similar situation to light. In the province of East Kalimantan there are at least twelve different groups who are known by the name Basap. Four of these are located in the Talisayan district, and they are socially culturally, and linguistically distinct from one another. One of these groups, residing in the forest hills above Teluk Sumbang, is nomadic. The other three are and, according to their traditions, always have been sedentary and agricultural. Six more Basap groups are to be found dispersed throughout the neighboring district of Sangkulirang. These again are separate from one another, but some are related to certain of the groups in Talisayan. The formerly nomadic Basap of Sandaran, for example, are in fact an extension of the nomadic Basap of the hills above Teluk Sumbang. The other Basap groups of the Sangkulirang district claim always to have been sedentary agriculturists.

Yet another group of Basap appears far to the north around the headwaters of the Birang River in the Gunung Tabor district. These people are nomadic and are a southern extension of the Punan Batu. Finally, there is a Basap group located far to the southwest at one village called Junggon in the district of Loa Kulu. Whereas I did not visit this group, I am uncertain as to its ethnic affiliation; the local government, however, classifies it as a branch of the Benuaq people. Thus here again we see a varied assortment of widely dispersed groups, of dissimilar origins, known by one common "ethnic" term.

Yet aside from their common label, these scattered groups do share in common the fact that they are located generally in coastal and near coastal districts of eastern Kalimantan, in a long swatch running from Tanjung Receb down to Samarinda. This seemed to me significant, so I began inquiring of peoples in this broad vicinity as to the meaning of the word Basap itself. As it happens, the denotative definition and etymology of the term have faded from memory, but the connotative meaning is clear. Among coastal Malays, Bugis, Banjars, and Bajaus resident in this general vicinity, Basap is simply synonymous with Dayak. These coastal "peoples of the sea," as I heard them describe themselves, use the word Basap to refer indiscriminately to what they perceive as "peoples of the land." Coastal peoples of Talisayan and Sangkulirang often use the words Basap and Dayak interchangeably when referring to the pagan indigenes of these areas. Moreover, in the coastal town of Biduk-Biduk I was asked by a young Buginese whether I had been to the interior of the island and had seen the Basap Kenyah. Let is be noted, finally, that the word Basap often has pejorative connotations in these districts and is resented by the peoples so-termed, who usually prefer to be called Dayaks.

Thus Murut, Tidong, Melanau, Kenyah, and Basap are but a few examples of the use of imprecise exonyms in Borneo and Dayak is another example, for that matter; Punan quite obviously is another. But what if anything, does the word Punan mean? There are, as always, several schools of thought on the subject.

Tom Harrisson was of the opinion that in many inland dialects of Borneo, particularly of Sarawak, the word punan means "upriver" or "headwaters of a river." As such, any group living in or around the upper reaches of a river would naturally be known as Orang Punan, or People from Upriver. As Harrisson stated the case, "Moreover, some people call anyone living in the headwaters of a river Punan. As between Radio Sarawak and the Sarawak Museum, R.S. is Punan and we at the S.M., 200 yards downwind of 'em, are not" (Harrison, 1959:136).

I.A.N. Urquhart, however, found that the Kenyah Nyamok, Kenyah Badang, Kenyah Leppo Aga, and the Sebup languages, or dialects, all have the word *mennan*, meaning "to stay in the jungle, a person who goes and lives in the jungle for two or three years and during that time does not plant crops." Urquhart came to believe that the ethnic name most likely derived from this word, and that the people probably descended from Kenyahs who went off into the jungle "for two or three years," and then simply stayed there (1959: passim).

Jerome Rousseau has observed:

> For a Kayan, the critical characteristic of "Punanhood" is nomadism: when I mentioned the presence of nomads in other parts of the world, the informants immediately classified them as "Punan," without asking about their culture, language, or physical characteristics. (Rousseau, 1975:45)

My own inquiries brought forth a somewhat different interpretation, but one that seems to complement these three nonetheless. I must say frankly, first of all, that few of the settled peoples, and none of the Punan groups I encountered had any idea at all as to the meaning and derivation of the word Punan (and no one at all could even imagine where the name Kenyah might have come from). Nevertheless, I did finally manage to discover that in two languages at least—Kenyah Lepo Tau and the Ot Danum dialect spoken along the upper Barito and Joloi rivers—*punan* has the meaning "to gather," "to collect," or "to assemble" things or goods.

As such, headwaters of a river, staying in the jungle, nomadism, and gathering, collecting, or assembling goods appear to be the basic elements of the connotative meaning of the word *punan*. The geographical, demographic, and occupational nature of the various renderings do much to suggest why so many different groups in Borneo have commonly been referred to as Punan; and it throws into new perspective the off hand remark once made to me by a young Kenyah, concerning the long-settled, village dwelling, completely agricultural Punan Oho: "They're not really Punan anymore, are they?"

Also thrown into new perspective are a couple of old, long-standing arguments. Forty years ago, as we saw in chapter 1, Fay-Cooper Cole was understood to say something to the effect of there being no such thing as the Punan, and he has been held up to ridicule ever since. This ridicule is undeserved. Let us review for a moment exactly what it was he did say:

> Despite the fact that people called Punan have been seen and reported by reliable parties I am still inclined to doubt their existence as a distinct people.
>
> I went to Borneo looking for Punan. While in Central Borneo I sought in vain for any such people, but I did find that any group which was away from home gathering jungle products and living in temporary camps was known as *punan*. I saw several such groups but upon inquiry found they all related to fixed villages. Under the circumstances I believe that in Central Borneo the term has no other significance than our word "camper." (Cole, 1947:340)

We are now, I think, able to appreciate just how close Cole came to making my fieldwork unnecessary. For he correctly perceived, albeit for the wrong reason, that groups called Punan are not a single, distinct people, and he displayed remarkable intuition with his reference to the gathering of jungle products. Cole's mistake was his failure to realize that these gathering groups—however much they indeed "related to fixed villages"—were not merely campers from these villages but full-time, specialized gathering groups.

We are perhaps now also better able to appreciate the enduring debate over whether the peoples dealt with in this study are properly to be called Punan or Penan. This debate, now well over thirty years old, resulted largely from Rodney Needham's study of certain nomadic and settled groups in Sarawak, whom he has said are called Penan. These people, he maintained, are completely distinct from nomadic Punan, who in turn are distinct from a sedentary agricultural longhouse people called the Punan Ba (Needham, 1954c; 1955; 1972). Despite Needham's firsthand observation that the Penan regard themselves as being separate, distinct, and different from the various nomadic groups known as Punan, other anthropologists have insisted that, Punan or Penan, these are all the same people, the two words reflecting nothing more than slight, insignificant phonological variations in the way different sedentary groups pronounce the nomads' name. As Harrisson so succinctly put it, "The fact is that the Kenyahs call them Penans, the Kayans call them Punans and they don't call *themselves* anything necessarily" (1959:136). Herbert Whittier (1974) has noted, moreover, that such phonological variation is likewise to be heard even within the different dialects of Kenyah alone. Some Kenyah, he says, refer to nomads as Punan while others employ the variant Penan.

The conclusion that emerges from the foregoing analysis, as far as this debate is concerned, is that Rodney Needham was right; and so were Harrisson and Whittier. For the two variant terms most likely *did* derive originally from phonological variation in the pronunciation of the one same word—whatever that word may have meant—and the Penan that Needham studied no doubt *are* distinct from the sedentary Punan Ba and groups of nomadic and settled Punan, just as all of these are distinct from one another.

4

Punan: Some Reflections

> The Phi Tong Luang live, surrounded by mystery, in the dense primeval forests of the mountain chain that emerges from the immense massif of Central Asia and extends southward between the broad valleys of the Mekong and Menam rivers. The Lao words, Phi Tong Luang, mean "Spirits of the Yellow Leaves," and the people are known in the region only by that name, for nothing is seen of them beyond hastily erected and soon abandoned windscreens occasionally found by hunters in the jungle. The withered foliage of the screens and the ashes of the people's fires give wide play to the fancy of the Lao in regard to the "spirits." What sort of creatures can they be, these people who so anxiously avoid all contact with other human beings, and who are able to exist in the depth of the wilderness, apparently always restlessly wandering, leaving their traces now in one place and now in another, so that their trail is more difficult to follow than those of wild animals? (Bernatzik, 1951:89)

This description of the nomadic Phi Tong Luang, or Yumbri, of the uplands of northeastern Thailand could, *mutatis mutandis*, easily pass muster as a typical early account of the Punan. In tone and viewpoint it is virtually identical to any one of several depictions of Punan appearing in the literature on Borneo.

Intrigued by rumors and vague reports heard among the lowland Lao, German ethnologist Hugo Adolf Bernatzik ascended to the hill country to find and observe these Spirits of the Yellow Leaves.

> We had ringing in our ears the scornful laughter of a European who had been settled for twenty-five years in that region: "You poor fools, I bet you a thousand to one you won't find the Phi Tong Luang." (Ibid.:90)

But find them he did and his subsequent description of them depicted a people who, by his accounts, appeared to be only barely human.

> From our large number of observations we were able to establish that the mental level of these primitives was far below that of the Moken or the Semang. The capacity for learning especially seems to be extraordinarily low . . . They are quite unable to grasp or learn

> anything quickly: this was evident again and again in connexion with all sorts of small duties new to them that were called for by our presence.
>
> We were unable to note any special faculties, such as inventiveness, commercial ability, organizing talent, or any sort of knowledge of nature .... (Ibid.: 126)

The Phi Tong Luang, according to Bernatzik, were in addition "incapable of abstract thought," "incapable of drawing conclusions," and "unable to talk about things of the past or the future"; they "had no conception of results till they appeared," "had no conception of cause and effect, and no capacity of intellectual assimilation of criticism." The Phi Tonk Luang, Bernatzik said, were also lacking the facility for memory: "If we casually made an appeal to their recollection we almost always received the reply: I don't know any longer," (ibid.: 127). Whereas Hose and McDougall had claimed (1912, II:211) that the Punan "do not count beyond three," Bernatzik offered that the Phi Tong Luang were unable to count at all, having in their language only two words to express quantity, meaning "much" and "few." Finally, it claimed that the Spirits of the Yellow Leaves, although nomadic, were not hunters and gatherers, but merely gatherers. They were restricted to gathering wild fruits and vegetables and foraging for snails, caterpillars, lizards, and other small animals that could be caught by hand on account of their lack of weapons and their total inability to use them (Bernatzik, 1951: 138–329, 162).

The conclusion that Bernatzik drew from all of this is that the Phi Tong Luang represented a tiny remnant of an aboriginal race, once widespread over Southeast Asia, that preceded even Negritos. "The Phi Tong Luang," Bernatzik said (ibid.: 166–37), "are the purest representatives among the peoples living today of the bearers of a presumably pre-neolithic wood or bamboo culture, and of a race of their own." As such they are, he said, "remnants of the old pre-negritic autochthonous population, which I may describe as protomongoloid. This oldest layer was later submerged under the waves of negritos, palaeoeuropids, and the palaeomongoloid races."

It has often been said that people believe what they want to believe, and Bernatzik clearly wanted to believe that he found a tiny remnant of the first Homo sapiens to appear in Southeast Asia. Having asked rhetorically "what sort of creatures" the Phi Tong Luang could be, he in effect answered his own question:

> With a limited, childish imagination, with their minds at work only on the needs of the moment, these relics of the remote past live in eternal fear of men and animals. How this people has been able, unarmed, to maintain its existence to this day will probably remain for all time a mystery of the immeasurable, impenetrable jungle, which brings down destruction on one but gives sanctuary to another. (Ibid.: 130)

In light of our foregoing discussion of the Punan, one wonders whether further study and analysis of the Phi Tong Luange might have shown that they were considerably less pristine or autochthonous than they ostensibly appeared. It is certain that further study would, if nothing else, have made these people to be substantially less of a "mystery of the immeasurable, impenetrable jungle." A careful perusal of Bernatzik's material brings forth the following noteworthy observations:

1. The photographs of the Phi Tong Luang that accompany the text show a people racially identical to the neighboring sedentary agricultural hill tribes. The nomads differ in appearance from the latter only in their lack of clothing, jewelry, and in their relative "unkemptness."
2. The map presented on page 88 showing the distribution of the various tribes in the region clearly indicates that specific Phi Tong Luang groups are located in close proximity to specific villages of the sedentary Kamuk and Meau peoples.
3. The rumors that initially had led Bernatzik to find and observe the Phi Tong Luang indicated that they were trading "beeswax, honey, and rattan" to the sedentary villagers in exchange for rice(Ibid:89).
4. Bernatzik was finally able to make contact with these people through assistance from a Chinese trader.

The last point merits attention. According to his account, Bernatzik encountered this trader while en route into the highlands to find the Phi Tong Luang. As he describes the fortuitous meeting:

> We were taken to a hut of bamboo and straw, on piles ten to a dozen feet high, and in no way different from the older dwellings of the Lao. We were received, however, in it by an old and very lean Chinese. He was sitting on the floor, smoking a long pipe, and stroked his thin imperial as he listened attentively to Bun Ma's exposition of our plans.
>
> He looked intelligent. What could he be doing in this remote jungle village? One usually finds Chinese only where there is money to be earned ....
>
> This man understood at once what we wanted, and said: "Three days' march from here, on the top of a mountain, is a Meau village that is frequently visited by Phi Tong Luang. The Meau headman, Tsin Tsai, is a friend of mine, and will arrange everything for you. I am in touch with the Phi Tong Luang through him. Look at those mats: they are the work of the 'Spirits' you want to find."
>
> He pointed to some rolls of matting, our first visible traces of the Phi Tong Luang.... (Ibid.: 97–98)

Bernatzik presents these revelations without further comment; their irony appears to have escaped him. The Chinese trader's mention of a Meau village "that is frequently visited by Phi Tong Luang" seems not to have shaken the author's conviction that the latter "anxiously avoid all contact with other human beings," and that "nothing is seen of them beyond hastily erected and soon abandoned windscreens occasionally found by hunters in the jungle" (ibid.: 89). Nor did Bernatzik attempt to reconcile his conception of "these relics of a remote past" (ibid.: 130) with his observations of an apparent trade network in forest products, involving the Phi Tong Luang, the sedentary Meau and Kamuk, and the Chinese trader. For Bernatzik, the Phi Tong Luang remained "surrounded by mystery, in the dense primeval forests . . . (ibid.: 89). There is, I think, an interesting study to be made concerning just what it is about the forests of Southeast Asia, and the inhabitants thereof, that western travelers seem to find so mysterious.

The similarities between this case of the Phi Tong Luang of Thailand and the Punan of Borneo are strikingly obvious. Not only are the style of reportage, the tone, and the underlying intellectual point of view identical to that found in so much of the literature on Punan, even relatively recent literature—(see chapter l), but the actual ethnographic situation appears to be the same as well. In both cases, we seem to be looking at a specific type of ecological adaptation. More to the point, we are dealing here with a specific form of hunting and gathering, one that is highly specialized and has little if anything to do with our usual conceptions of generalized, unilinear social evolution.

In 1968 a milestone event occurred in the anthropological study of hunters and gatherers. This entailed the publication in that year of *Man the Hunter* (Lee and Devore, eds.), a major collection of short research papers and round-table discussions on the cross-cultural study of hunting and gathering as a phase of human evolution, and as a way of life. The overall impact of this volume has been immeasurable. As a state-of-the-art compendium on hunting and gathering, it rapidly became staple feature in undergraduate reading lists and an almost inevitable contribution to undergraduate training in anthropology. For many of us trained as anthropologists in American universities in the 1970's, *Man the Hunter* was both a touchstone and fact of life.

The book itself was the result of a symposium held two years earlier, at which some seventy-five scholars from around the world met to share information on hunting and gathering peoples of both the ethnographic present and the prehistoric past. In addition to social anthropologists, physical anthropologists, and specialists in demography, ecology, and human ethology. The intent of the symposium was to synthesize the available data on hunters and gatherers, not only to explicate various ethnographic issues but also to shed new light on hunting and gathering as a once universal stage in the evolution of man. Thus for most of the symposium's participants, the study of present day groups of hunters and gatherers was perceived as a crucial means toward understanding and illuminating mankind's universal hunting and gathering past (Lee and DeVore, 1968:3). Perhaps the most eloquent statement of this perception was that expressed by George Murdock:

> Ten thousand years ago the entire population of the earth subsisted by hunting and gathering, as their ancestors had done since the dawn of culture. By the time of Christ, eight thousand years later, tillers and herders had replaced them over at least half of the earth. At the time of the discovery of the New World, only perhaps 15 percent of the earth's surface was still occupied by hunters and gatherers, and this area has continued to decline at a progressive rate until the present day, when only a few isolated pockets survive.
>
> Many of the peoples who subsisted by hunting and gathering at the time of Columbus have disappeared entirely and been replaced by stronger peoples. Others have been reduced to dependency—on reservations or as servants or outcaste groups. Still others have made a transition, in some form or another, to modes or subsistence based on agriculture, animal husbandry, or industrial employment. Only a handful still live an independent life of hunting and gathering, nearly all of them under markedly altered conditions. It is time—indeed, long past time—that we took stock of these dwindling remnants, for it is among them that we can still study at first hand the modes of life and types of cultural adjustments that prevailed throughout most of human history. (Murdock, 1968:13)

Judging from the resulting volume *Man the Hunter*, Murdock seems to have been stating what evidently was the majority opinion of the symposium's participants—an almost a priori notion that present day groups of hunters and gatherers are "dwindling remnants" of the once universal paleolithic phase of human evolution, and that they comprise "isolated pockets" of humankind's preneolithic, pre-agricultural past.

This symposium was remarkable, however, in its diversity of expertise. Not only did its participants synthesize data on hunters and gatherers, a few also raised such provocative questions as whether hunters and gatherers truly represent a uniform cultural type. Others, more significantly, introduced readers like myself to the observation that some nomadic groups of the present day are in fact the result of a "readaptation" (Lee and DeVore, 1968:4) to hunting and gathering, having derived originally from sedentary agricultural peoples. This was essentially the contribution of Donald Lathrap, who cited as his example the hunting and gathering peoples of the tropical forest zone of South America:

> Most of the primitive groups inhabiting the tropical forest uplands away from the major flood plains can be interpreted as the wreckage of evolved agricultural societies forced into an environment unsuitable to the basic economic pattern. Deprived of the riverine resources, such groups had to rely on the hunting of forest game to provide the protein and fat essential to the diet. A more intense orientation to hunting the relatively scarce game available led to more nomadism, a decline in agricultural productivity, and a still greater dependence on wild food....

> The speed with which this kind of cultural devolution can take place is suggested by the relatively minor linguistic differences between the riverine Panoans such as the Shipibo and Conibo and the very "primitive" interfluvial Panoan groups such as the Cashibo and Remo.
>
> While the "hunting" cultures of the tropical forest zone of South America offer highly explicit examples of the cultural and demographic effects of a dependence on hunting in an area where hunting is neither profitable or easy, they probably instruct us not at all about the nature of pre-Neolithic hunting cultures. (Lathrap, 1968:29).

Thus the symposium and the resultant compendium *Man the Hunter* have left some significant epistemological imprints. The basic, widespread conception that modern day hunters and gatherers are vanishing relics of the paleolithic was codified and perpetuated. A minority opinion that some hunters and gatherers derive from sedentary agriculturalists was established and disseminated amongst a large audience of readers. A third and somewhat unfortunate effect, however, was the depiction of this latter class of hunters and gatherers as "failed agriculturalists." As expressed by the volume's editors,

> A further consideration was introduced by Lathrap (Chapter 3) and others who cited a number of hunting peoples who were "failed" agriculturalists. The *readaptation* to hunting, or "devolution" as it has been called, characterized such classic "hunters" as the Siriono of South America and the Veddas of Ceylon. (Lee and DeVore, 1968:4)

Let us indeed consider the case of the Veddas of Ceylon. While there is probably little doubt that these people did in fact derive from sedentary, agricultural Sinhalese at some time in the past, there is, I think, no good reason to suspect that failure or devolution had anything to do with their readaption to hunting and gathering. A brief examination of the Seligmanns' prodigious ethnographic reconstruction of the Veddas is repaid with such notable observations as these:

> The wilder Veddas of those days built no houses but lived entirely in caves; trading places called *wadia* near the caves, but out of sight of them, under a tree or rock, were used for bartering, where all strangers would stop and shout and then wait until their calls had been answered from the caves. (Seligmann and Seligmann, 1911:32–33)

> A few necessities of life which the forest does not supply, such as steel and iron for their arrowheads and axes, and the very scanty clothing which they wear, they obtain by barter, their wax, and honey, elk flesh and ivory, being eagerly sought after by the neighbouring Sinhalese. (Ibid.: 94)

These observations should, by now, have a familiar ring. The picture that emerges is not one of cultural retrogression but of economic specialization. We are dealing here with people not unlike the Punan, who, rather than being the wreckage of sedentary societies, appear to be descendents of people who opted to specialize in the collection of resources that could best be obtained through full time nomadism in primary forest areas. Whereas it evidently occurred to some Dayak groups in the past that it was more efficient to have two types of people exploiting two different niches than to have one type of people exploiting both, I see no reason to believe that people elsewhere in the world have been any less inventive.

There is perhaps no more illustrative example of economic specialization at the group level in which hunters and gatherers were involved, than that which prevailed in the Nilgiri Hills in South India at the time of Rivers' classic study (1906). There on the same plateau lived the pastoral Todas, the agricultural Badags, and the artisan Kotas, along with what Rivers called "two wild, dwarfish tribes" (ibid.: 6) of hunters and gatherers—the Irulas and Kurumbas, ranging through the plateau's forested slopes. Living together in close economic symbiosis, these tribes presented what for all intents and purposes was a caste system, with accompanying *jajmani* relationships, without the overarching ideology of Hinduism. Here again, one can only wonder to what extent the wildness and dwarfishness of the Irulas and Kurumbas was real or simply in the eye of a western observer.

What this all boils down to perhaps, is the suggestion that we ought to reexamine the ethnographic record and draw a distinction between two different types of hunters and gatherers. While doing this, we might also draw a very necessary distinction between two quite different types of hunting and gathering adaptations.

The first distinction, that between the two types of hunters and gatherers, involves recognizing the difference between what may be termed primary hunters and gatherers on the one hand and secondary hunters and gatherers on the other. Primary hunters and gatherers are those groups who would in fact appear to be the aboriginal, autochthonous peoples of their respective regions, groups for whom no evidence whatsoever exists of a prior agricultural adaptation. This type would include such well known examples as the Andaman Islanders, the Semang of Malaysia, and Pygmy peoples of central Africa, and the Australian aborigines, among others.

Secondary hunters and gatherers are those groups that clearly appear to derive—not devolve—from sedentary agricultural peoples. These are groups for whom hunting and gathering is essentially a readaptation toward a specialized ecological niche. Some examples of this type would be the Punan of Borneo, other nomadic groups of Borneo known by different names, the Phi Tong Luang of northeastern Thailand, the Kubu of Sumatra, the Tasaday of Mindanao, perhaps most of the hunting and gathering groups of the Indian subcontinent, the Veddas of Ceylon, as well as most if not all of the hunting and gathering peoples of the tropical forest zone of South America.

Under no circumstances should this distinction between primary and secondary hunters and gatherers be interpreted to imply, even faintly, a distinction between "real" hunters and gatherers and groups that are somehow "unreal" or "impure." Such a perspective would be quite counterproductive, and it is in no way suggested by the present study. The fact that a hunting and gathering group appears to derive from a former sedentary agricultural adaptation does not mean that it is in any way less genuine, less interesting, or less instructive with respect to hunting and gathering as a way of life.

The second distinction that ought to be drawn is that which differentiates between what are really two quite different types of hunting and gathering adaptations: subsistence hunting and gathering on the one hand, and what has been called commercial hunting and gathering on the other. Subsistence hunting and gathering is the type that prevailed universally throughout the paleolithic, and which we have seen in modern times among such groups as the Andaman Islanders and the aborigines of Australia. Commercial hunting and gathering, in which the collection of commodities for trade forms a major, if not primary motivation for nomadism, may well be found to account for the majority of hunting and gathering groups of the ethnographic present.

> We have seen how the Europeans in Sarawak history have tried to impose their own ideas of bounded, permanent and stable ethnic identity on the very different Sarawak scene. The Brookes did their best to keep various peoples separate, to make neat and tidy categories that were more in keeping with their orderly British minds.
>
> Indigenous ethnicity, unlike racial identity, was not held to be immutable, and indeed was characterized by impermanence. If we are to have an accurate understanding of traditional Borneo, we must form a picture of populations continually "becoming" something else, a picture with very few solid lines demarcating ethnic boundaries. (Babcock, 1974:196–97)

> [A]nthropologists have reasoned from a misleading idea of the prototype inter-ethnic situation. One has tended to think in terms of different peoples, with different histories and cultures, coming together and accommodating themselves to each other, generally in a colonial setting. To visualize the basic requirements for the co-existence of ethnic diversity, I would suggest that we rather ask ourselves what is needed to make ethnic distinctions *emerge* in an area. (Barth, 1969:17)

Certain further lines of inquiry are suggested by the foregoing analysis of hunting and gathering in Borneo. It has been the contention of this study that the existence of Punan groups in Borneo arose initially from the demand for various jungle products desired by Chinese. As such, a significant problem relating to the emergence of these groups is the economic basis of ethnicity. Without having to stray too far from the subject of this monograph, we may consider some other instances in which economic stimuli led to the creation of nomadic groups elsewhere in the world.

We know for example that it was a combination of population pressures and the introduction of the horse that caused various settled agricultural groups to abandon their villages on the prairie and move out onto the Great Plains of North America. These groups, erstwhile village dwelling farmers, adopted a specialized hunting adaptation during the late eighteenth and early nineteenth centuries, while accepting and developing such new cultural traits as the sun dance, coup counting warfare, intratribal associations, and paramount chieftainship. We have specific historical information, such as that concerning one group which in effect bifurcated: one segment remaining sedentary and agricultural, and known to us as the Hidatsa; the other becoming mounted, buffalo hunting nomads, known to us as the Crows. And we know moreover that the two now-distinct "tribes" remained in close association, trading with each other and maintaining an economic symbiosis (cf. Lowie, 1963; Meyer, 1977).

With respect to the Near East, we have an interesting synthesis by Brian Spooner (1973) in which the point is argued that pastoral nomadism similarly derives from a sedentary agricultural adaptation. Spooner demonstrates various ecological and economic factors that have led to the present sociocultural distinction between nomadic Arab bedouins and sedentary Arab peasants.

I believe that the case of the Punan of Borneo may be construed as a further example of the economic basis for ethnic differentiation, and as a point of departure for further studies in this vein involving hunters and gatherers specifically.

Another line of inquiry suggested by the present analysis concerns the historical development of insular Southeast Asia, in which Borneo appears to have played a significant part. It is time for anthropologists to stop thinking of Borneo as though it were another New Guinea. While the remote interior of the latter island was indeed inhabited by culturally isolated peoples, some of whom remained uncontacted and undisturbed by outside influences until well into the present century, the ethnographic situation in Borneo presents quite another picture.

Since the earliest centuries of the present millennium, the island of Borneo has been a heavily trafficked and well-trodden crossroads for many of the major civilizations of the East. Borneo and its peoples have played host to Chinese, Indians, Arabs, and Persians, as well as peninsular and littoral Malays. A Bornean kingdom sent tribute to the court of China as early as A.D. 977, and it did so through the employment of three Arab envoys (Purcell, 1951:25). Bornean kingdoms established contacts with the Indonesian empires of Srivijaya and Madjapahit and Borneo sultanates later waged wars and forged alliances with those of the Sulu Sea. Borneo and its peoples have been part of the larger world.

O.W. Wolters (1967) has shown in lengthy and meticulous detail that the kingdom of Srivijaya, on the island of Sumatra, developed into statehood from its role as a major commodities entrepot for the China trade. An even earlier kingdom, indeed *the earliest* known Indonesian kingdom, was that of Kutai in eastern Borneo. This fifth century kingdom was situated at the lower reaches of the Mahakam River, where, as we have seen in modern times,

> The produce of the country . . . is brought down the river on long rafts. Rattan is the staple product; but gutta percha, timber, beeswax, and edible birds' nests (*Sarong boreroeng*) from the interior, and trepang, tortoise shell, and turtle eggs from the coast, are also exported in considerable quantities. (Bock, 1882: 25–26)

It may of course be purely coincidental, but one cannot help but notice that the two islands that provided the setting for the earliest Indonesian kingdoms are the same two islands in Indonesia on which may be found full time, specialized nomadic hunting and gathering groups collecting forest products for trade. A particularly intriguing question is thus the extent to which hunters and gatherers may have contributed, however unknowingly, to the formation and maintenance of complex states.

Bibliography

Alexander, Garth. 1973. *The Invisible China; the Overseas Chinese and the Politics of Southeast Asia.* New York: Macmillan.

Andreini, E.L. 1924. "The Gypsies of Sarawak (Punans)." *Journal of the Malayan Branch of the Royal Asiatic Society* II:76–77.

Appell, George. 1976. Introduction to *The Societies of Borneo; Explorations in the Theory of Cognatic Social Structure* (Appell, ed.). Washington, D.C.: American Anthropological Association, Special Publishers Number Six.

______. 1982. "Ethnic Groups in the Northeast Region of Indonesian Borneo and their Social Organization." Paper presented at the 81st annual meeting of the American Anthropological Association, Washington, D.C.

Ave, J.B. 1972. "Kalimantan Dayaks." In *Ethnic Groups of Insular Southeast Asia*, I, pp.185–87, edited by Frank LeBar. New Haven: Human Relations Area Files Press.

Babcock, Tim G. 1974. "Indigenous Ethnicity in Sarawak." *Sarawak Museum Journal* XXII:191–202.

Barth, Fredrik. 1969. Introduction to *Ethnic Groups and Boundaries; the Social Organization of Culture Difference.* (Barth, ed): Boston: Little, Brown and Company, pp. 9–38.

Beccari, Odoardo. 1904. *Wanderings in the Great Forest of Borneo.* London: Archibald Constable and Co.

Beech, Mervyn W.H. 1911. "Punans of Borneo." *Man* XI:17–18.

Beeckman, Daniel. 1718. *A Voyage to and from the Island of Borneo in the East-Indies.* Reprinted 1973. Folkstone (Kent, England): Dawson of Pall Mall.

Bock, Carl. 1882. *The Head-Hunters of Borneo; a Narrative of Travel up the Mahakkam and down the Barito.* London: Sampson Low, Marston, Searle and Rivington.

Bernatzik, Hugo Adolf. 1951. *The Spirits of the Yellow Leaves.* London: Robert Hale.

Blundell, Peter. 1923. *The City of Many Waters.* London: Arrowsmith.

Blust, Robert A. 1972. "Report of Linguistic Field Work Undertaken in Sarawak." *Borneo Research Bulletin* IV:12–14.

______. 1976. "Austronesian Culture History: Some Linguistic Inferences and the Relations to the Archaeological Record." *World Archaeology* VIII, 1:19–43.

Braddell, Sir Roland. 1941. "An Introduction to the Study of Ancient Times in the Malay Peninsula and the Straits of Malacca." *Journal of the Malayan Branch of the Royal Asiatic Society*, XIX, 1:72.

______. 1949a. "A Note on Sambas and Borneo." *Journal of the Malayan Branch of the Royal Asiatic Society* XXII, 4:1–12.

______. 1949b. "P'o-li in Borneo." *Sarawak Museum Journal* I:5–9.

Bretschneider, E. 1871. *On the Knowledge Possessed by the Ancient Chinese of the Arabs and Arabian Colonies and other Western Countries Mentioned in Chinese Books.* London.

Brooke, Charles. 1866. *Ten Years in Sarawak*. 2 vols. London: Tinsley Brothers.

Cheng, Te-K' un. 1969. *Archaeology in Sarawak*. Cambridge: W. Heffer and Sons.

Cole, Fay Cooper. 1945. *The Peoples of Malaysia*. Princeton, N.J.: Van Nostrand.

———. 1947. "Concerning the Punan of Borneo." *American Anthropologists*, SLIX:340.

Conley, William. 1973. *The Kalimantan Kenyah: A study of Tribal Conversion in terms of Dynamic-Cultural Themes*. Pasadena: Fuller Theological Seminary.

Dalton, Bill. 1977. *Indonesia Handbook*. Franklin Village, Mich. Moon Publications.

Dove, Michael. 1980. "Swidden Systems, and their Potential Role in Agricultural Development: A Case Study from Kalimantan." Manuscript.

Harrisson, Tom. 1949. "Notes on some Nomadic Punans." *Sarawak Museum Journal* V:130–146.

———. 1959. *The Peoples of Sarawak*. Kuching: Sarawak Museum.

———. 1975. "Further Notes on Sarawak and Kalimantan Punan (and Penan)." *Borneo Research Bulletin* VII, 1:3–4.

Heine Geldern, Robert. 1945. *Prehistoric Research in the Netherlands Indies*. New York: Southeast Asia Institute.

———. 1946. "Research on Southeast Asia: Problems and Suggestions." *American Anthropologist* XLVIII:149–175.

Holmberg, Allan R. 1950. *Nomads of the Long Bow, the Siriono of Eastern Bolivia*. Washington, D.C.: Smithsonian Institution, Institute of Social Anthropology, Publication Number Ten.

Hornaday, William T. 1894. *Two Years in the Jungle: The Experiences of a Hunter and Naturalist*. New York: Charles Scribner's Sons.

Hose, Charles. 1893. "The Natives of Borneo." *Journal of the Royal Anthropological Institute* XXIII:156–172.

Hose, Charles and McDougall, William. 1912. *The Pegan Tribes of Borneo*. 2 Vols. London: Macmillan.

King, Victor. 1974. "Notes on Punan and Bukat in West Kalimantan." *Borneo Research Bulletin* VI 2:39–42.

Krohn, William O. 1927. *In Borneo Jungles; Among the Dyak Headhunters*. Indianapolis: Bobbs Merrill.

Krom, J.S. 1939. "Berau Monography." Manuscript.

Langub, Jayl. 1975. "Distribution of Penan and Punan in the Belaga District." *Borneo Research Bulletin* VII, 2:45–48.

Lathrap, Donald W. 1968. "The 'Hunting' Economies of the Tropical Forest Zone of South America: An Attempt at Historical Perspective." In *Man the Hunter*, Richard B. Lee and Irven DeVore (eds), pp. 23–29. Chicago: Aldine.

LeBar, Frank, ed. 1972. *Ethnic Groups of Insular Southeast Asia*. Vol I. New Haven: Human Relations Area Files Press.

Lee, Richard B. and DeVore, Irven, eds. 1968. *Man the Hunter*. Chicago: Aldine.

Low, Sir Hugh. 1848. *Sarawak; Its Inhabitants and Productions: Being Notes During a Residence in that Country with H.H. The Rajah Brooke*. London: Richard Bentley.

———. 1893. Discussion of "The Natives of Borneo," by Charles Hose. *Journal of the Royal Anthropological Institute* XXIII:171–172.

Lowie, Robert. 1963. *Indians of the Plains*. New York: American Museum Science Books.

Meyer, Roy W. 1977. *The Village Indians of the Upper Missouri; the Mandans, Hidatsas, and Arikaras*. Lincoln, Neb. University of Nebraska Press.

Miller, Charles, C. 1942. *Black Borneo*. New York: Modern Age Books.

Murdock, George P. 1968. "The Current Status of the World's Hunting and Gathering Peoples." In *Man the Hunter*, Richard B. Lee and Irven DeVore (eds.), pp. 13–20. Chicago: Aldine.

Needham, Rodney. 1954a. "The System of Teknonyms and Death-Names of the Penant." *Southwestern Journal of Anthropology* X:416–431.

______. 1954b. "Siriono and Penan: A Test of Some Hypotheses." *Southwestern Journal of Anthropology* X:228–232.

______. 1954c. "Penan and Punan." *Journal of the Malayan Branch of the Royal Asiatic Society*, XXVII, 1:73–83.

______. 1955. "Punan Ba." *Journal of the Malayan Branch of the Royal Asiatic Society* XXVIII, 1:24–36.

______. 1964. "Blood, Thunder, and Mockery of Animals." *Sociologus* (new series) XIV, 2:136–149.

______. 1965. "Death-Names and Solidarity in Penan Society." *Bijdragen tot de Taal-, Land- en Volkenkunde* CXXI:58–76.

______. 1971. "Penan Friendship-Names." In *The Translation of Culture*, Thomas O. Beidelman (ed.), pp. 203–230. London: Tavistock.

______. 1972. "Penan." In *Ethnic Groups of Insular Southeast Asia*, Frank LeBar (ed.), I: pp. 176–800. New Haven: Human Relations Area Files Press.

Pemerinta Daerah Kabupaten Kutai (Government of the Kutai Regency). 1974. *Kabupaten Kutai Dalam Masa Pelita-I.* Tenggarong and Samarinda, Kalimantan Timur, Indonesia.

Peranio, Roger D. 1972. "Bisayo." In *Ethnic Groups of Insular Southeast Asia*, I, pp. 163–660. New Haven: Human Relations Area Files Press.

Prentice, D.J. 1972. "Idahan Murut." In *Ethnic Groups of Insular Southeast Asia*, I, pp. 154–580. Frank LeBar (ed.). New Haven: Human Relations Area Files Press.

Purcell, Victor. 1951. *The Chinese in Southeast Asia.* Oxford: Oxford University Press.

Rivers, W.H.R. 1906. *The Todas.* London: Macmillan.

Rousseau, Jerome. 1975. "Ethnic Identity and Social Relations in Central Borneo." *Contributions to Asian Studies* VII:32–49.

Rubenstein, Carol. 1973. *Poems of the Indigenous Peoples of Sarawak: Some of the Songs and Chants. Sarawak Museum Journal* XXI, 42, part two; issued as *Sarawak Museum Journal,* Special Monograph Number Two.

Runciman, Steven. 1960. *The White Rajahs; a History of Sarawak from 1841 to 1946.* Cambridge: Cambridge University Press.

St. John, Spenser. 1862. *Life in the Forest of the Far East.* 2 vols. London: Smith, Elder and Co.

Sather, Clifford. 1972. "Tidong." In *Ethnic Groups of Insular Southeast Asia*, Frank LeBar (ed.) I, pp. 167–68. New Haven: Human Relations Area Files Press.

Scharer, Hans. 1963. *Ngaju Religion; the Conception of God among a South Borneo People.* The Hague: Martinus Nijhoff.

Seligmann, C.G. and Seligmann, B.Z. 1911. *The Veddas.* Cambridge: Cambridge University Press.

Spaen, A.H. 1901. "Een Reis naar de Binnenlanden van Borneo, 26 Aug. - 17 Sept. 1901." Manuscript.

Spooner, Brian. 1973. *The Cultural Ecology of Pastoral Nomads.* An Addison-Wesley Module in Anthropology, Number 45, Reading, Mass.: Addison-Wesley.

Turnbull, Colin M. 1965. *Wayward Servants, the Two Worlds of the African Pygmies.* Garden City: Natural History Press.

Urquhart, I.A.N. 1957. "Some Kenyah-Pennan Relationships." *Sarawak Museum Journal,* VIII:113–116.

______. 1959. "Nomadic Punans." In *The Peoples of Sarawak*, Tom Harrisson (ed.), pp. 73–83. Kuching: Sarawak Museum.

Wang, Gungwu. 1958. "The Nanhai Trade; a Study of the Early History of Chinese Trade in the South China Sea." *Journal of the Malayan Branch of the Royal Asiatic Society* XXXI, 2:1-133.

Wheatley, Paul. 1959. "Geographical Notes on some Commodities Involved in Sung Maritime Trade." *Journal of the Malayan Branch of the Royal Asiatic Society* XXXII, 2:5–140.

Whittier, Herbert L. 1973. *Social Organization and Symbols of Social Differentiation: An Ethnographic Study of the Kenyah Dayak of East Kalimantan (Borneo).* Ann Arbor: University Microfilms.

———. 1974. "The Distribution of Punan in East Kalimantan." *Borneo Research Bulletin* VI, 2:42–48.

Wolters, O.W. 1967. *Early Indonesian Commerce: A Study of the Origins of Srivijaya.* Ithaca: Cornell University Press.

Wright, Eugene. 1928. *The Great Horn Spoon.* Indianapolis: Bobbs-Merrill.

Index